POWERFUL STRUGGLES

Managing Resistance, Building Rapport

by

John W. Maag, Ph.D.

ISBN #1-57035-505-3

Edited by Francelia Sevin

Text layout and design by Maria McGrorey

Illustration by Larry Nolte

05 04 03 02 01   6 5 4 3 2 1

Post-it Notes is a registered trademark of Minnesota Mining and Manufacturing Company (3M).

Printed in the United States of America

Published and Distributed by

SOPRIS
WEST

4093 Specialty Place Longmont, Colorado 80504

(303) 651-2829 www.sopriswest.com

(149RESIST/BAN/5-01/5M/2.13)

Dedication

This book is dedicated to all the children

who challenged me to be creative and "think outside of the box."

About the Author

John W. Maag, Ph.D., a professor at the University of Nebraska-Lincoln, specializes in the education and treatment of children and adolescents with emotional and behavioral disorders. He is a nationally recognized behavioral consultant to agencies, school districts, and organizations on best practices for managing resistance and improving relationships. Dr. Maag's research interests include the study of effective self-management techniques, use of functional assessment, development of comprehensive behavior management programs, and the treatment of depression and attention deficit disorders. He has published more than 70 articles and book chapters and is the author of *Parenting without Punishment* (Charles Press), a Parent's Choice award-winner. A licensed psychotherapist, Dr. Maag is a frequent public speaker and a consulting editor to numerous journals.

Contents

ix   Preface

1   Part I: The Nature of Resistance

3   Chapter 1: The Role of Paradigms

9   Chapter 2: Understanding Resistance

15   Chapter 3: The Nature of Rapport

19   Part II: From Child to Context

21   Chapter 4: Two Models for Working with Resistance

27   Chapter 5: Helping Students Who Lack the Necessary Skills (a Type 1 Prerequisite)

39   Chapter 6: Helping Students Who Have Pessimistic Expectations or Anxious Thoughts (a Type 2 Prerequisite)

51   Part III: Function Over Form

53   Chapter 7: The Impact of Environment on Behavior

57   Chapter 8: Antecedent Manipulations

67   Chapter 9: Consequent Manipulations

85   Chapter 10: Conducting Functional Assessments

97   Part IV: Changing *Our* Behavior

99   Chapter 11: Overcoming Limitations

105   Chapter 12: Strategies for Controlling Our Emotions and Behaviors

115   Chapter 13: Advanced Approaches for Managing Resistance

147   Conclusion

151   References

155   Reproducibles

175   Index

Preface

The purpose of this book is to provide a conceptualization of the nature, cause, and treatment of resistance (noncompliance, disobedience to directions, uncooperative behaviors, and opposition). This book challenges the notion that resistance resides in students. It is our behaviors as educators that create resistance. Do you disagree with me? If so, then I have just created your resistance!

The assertion that our behaviors create resistance carries with it both good news and bad news. The good news is that because resistance originates from us, its management is completely within our control. The bad news is that it is difficult for us to change *our* own behaviors.

One of the most challenging experiences we face as educators is managing student resistance. Resistance can take the form of noncompliance, disobedience to directions, uncooperative behaviors, and opposition. Most interventions to address resistance typically focus on modifying student behaviors. Student behaviors are seen as the source of the problem. However, Walker, Colvin, and Ramsey (1995) insightfully noted that "whether or not a child complies with an adult directive has as much to do with how the command is framed and delivered as it does with the consequences, or lack of them, that follow the delivery" (p. 399). They go on to describe the difference between alpha and beta commands:

> **Alpha commands** are given in a clear, direct, and specific manner with few verbalizations and allow a reasonable time for compliance to occur.

> **Beta commands** are vague, overly wordy, and often contain multiple instructions.

The implication of these terms is that student resistance may either be exacerbated or alleviated by adult behaviors.

Most interventions that do include modification of adult behaviors generally focus on maximizing the use of alpha commands. What is often lost in these approaches is that many adult behaviors (threatening, pleading, insisting, and being domineering) can spawn noncompliance in students. In fact, Cormier and Cormier (1985) stated that resistance can arise from any behavior that interferes with the likelihood of a successful outcome being obtained—regardless of the source. In their definition, Cormier and Cormier provide the rationale for using the term **resistance** instead of the more common words **noncompliance** and **opposition**. The term "resistance" focuses on the interaction between adult behaviors and the behaviors of children, while "noncompliance" and "opposition" suggest that the problem resides solely with children.

Part I of this book discusses how we conceptualize resistance. Specifically, it sheds light on the paradigm from which we operate and its impact on which techniques are available for managing resistance. Part I concludes with a discussion of the nature of rapport—the opposite of resistance—based on the work of Milton H. Erickson, M.D.

Part II argues that resistance does not originate from some disorder inherent in a child but is due rather to the absence of requisite skills.

Environmental factors that are essential to the management of resistance are described in **Part III**. This section stresses the importance of restructuring interactions with peers, finding effective and alternative reinforcers, manipulating context, and conducting functional assessments. Reinforcement is conceptualized as an *effect,* rather than a *thing*. In other words, reinforcement is defined based on its function.

Part IV delves into resistance due to adult factors. Not only does it offer techniques, but it also investigates how we can change our mindsets and adopt new patterns of behavior. It reinforces, and elaborates on, the information and techniques presented in the previous parts.

Some of the information and techniques presented in Parts II, III, and IV overlap. For example, how we proceed to make a small change in our behavior in Part II is similar to the techniques used in Part III to change student patterns or routines. This overlap is intentional. This common thread helps us develop the overall conceptual "roadmap" for managing resistance.

Much of this book is based on the work of Milton H. Erickson, M.D., the foremost expert on clinical hypnosis and developer of strategic therapy. Since Erickson's death in 1980, strategic therapy has increased in popularity worldwide. In strategic therapy, therapists take responsibility for directly influencing their clients. The strategic therapist identifies solvable problems, sets goals, designs approaches for each problem, and examines the client's responses in order to make corrections and achieve goals. Haley (1993) acknowledged that it is difficult to describe Erickson's work because it blurs the line between scientist, healer, and poet. In addition, Erickson disdained the "Procrustean bed of hypothetical theory," preferring to formulate treatments based on individuals' unique characteristics. That is not to say that all of his techniques are idiosyncratic. For example, his use of paradoxical directives has been advocated by professionals from such diverse backgrounds as psychoanalysis and behaviorism. However, it was Erickson's unique way of applying these techniques that set him apart from other clinicians. I have drawn from his approach to therapy and his techniques for promoting change throughout this book.

PART I

The Nature of Resistance

Chapter 1

The Role of Paradigms

What has four wheels and flies?

What is green all over and has wheels?

What do Alexander the Great and Smokey the Bear have in common?

You may be asking, "What in the world do these riddles have to do with managing resistance?" The answer is that riddles force us to view things from alternative perspectives. Riddles take us out of our normal paradigms, or viewpoints. (Don't worry about the answers to the riddles, they appear in the Conclusion.)

We all have our own reality of which we try to convince others. This is the paradigm we operate from—our thoughts, perceptions, and values that form our particular vision of reality. Information from the environment is filtered through our human senses and finds its way into our minds where we make it into perceptions and thoughts. The byproduct of this process—knowledge—is influenced, in part, by social and cultural contexts. It is also shaped by how we perceive and process information within the constraints of our belief systems.

One example of how our beliefs affect what we perceive is found in eyewitness accounts of crimes. Fleeting impressions are elaborated on by individuals into complete accounts that they believe to be true. Events are construed in ways that are consistent with the observer's emotions and prejudices. As a result, people may be erroneously identified as the perpetrators. When such events are videotaped and reviewed repeatedly by people who were not at the crime scene, a different consensus of the event emerges; one that is not always consistent with eyewitness accounts. Eyewitnesses to a crime, or other emotional events, glean only partial knowledge from the immediate experience. They fill in the gaps in their knowledge by plausible constructions of what "must have" or "should have" happened in order to make sense of the scene.

Like the observers of a crime, each of us approaches problems with a unique theoretical viewpoint or paradigm—whether explicit or implicit—that enables us to interpret information. In other words, paradigms provide a set of rules for making sense of our environment. In his book *The Structure of Scientific Revolutions*, Kuhn (1970) discovered that paradigms acted as filters that screened the data coming into scientists' minds. Data that agreed with scientists' paradigms were easily recognized and accepted. Conversely, data that did not match the scientists' expectations, i.e., that did not fit their paradigms, caused substantial difficulty. In fact, the more unexpected the data, the more trouble scientists had perceiving and accepting them. In some cases, scientists simply ignored unexpected data. Other times, they ended up distorting the data to fit their paradigm rather than acknowledging the data as exceptions to the rules. In extreme cases, Kuhn found that scientists were simply incapable of perceiving the unexpected data—for all intents and purposes the data were invisible!

Figure 1-1
The Rubin Vase.
Note. From *Sensation and Perception*, Second Edition (p. 291), by Coren, S.; Porac, C.; and Ward., L.M., 1984, Orlando, FL: Harcourt. Reprinted with permission.

Like the scientists in Kuhn's study, we constantly select from the world those data that best fit our rules and regulations, while trying to ignore the rest. As a result, what may be perfectly obvious to a person adhering to one paradigm may be totally imperceptible to a person with a different paradigm. Gestalt and perception psychologists have, perhaps somewhat unknowingly, provided interesting data on the effect of one's paradigm. Take, for example, research on the "figure-ground" phenomenon—the mind's ability to focus attention on a meaningful pattern and ignore the rest of the data. In 1915, psychologist Edgar Rubin used a number of test patterns to assess individuals' figure-ground perception. The most famous of these test patterns is the Rubin vase (*Figure 1-1*).

If we look at the Rubin vase, we do not see the background and if we look at the background—two faces in profile—we do not see the vase. Moreover, we can seemingly will ourselves to see whichever we choose.

Another example of a paradigm is the classic one by Boring, created in 1930. In *Figure 1-2* do you see a young woman or an old lady? Your answer depends on what you choose to see.

Paradigms and Resistance

So, what do paradigms have to do with managing resistance? Because the dominant paradigm regarding resistance is that resistance originates from the student, we believe that resistance can be eliminated if we can get the student to perform the desired behavior. Consequently, methods for managing resistance are sought that conform to this paradigm. Viewing the management of resistance from this single perspective limits our ability to perceive alternative solutions. This results in a particularly deleterious condition called "para-

Figure 1-2
Boring's famous perceptual test. *Note.* From *A History of Experimental Psychology* (second edition), by Boring, E.G. 1950, New York: Appleton-Century-Crafts.

digm paralysis"—a disorder of terminal certainty! Individuals who suffer from this disorder will have an extremely difficult time managing resistance. They will continue to use the same tactics for handling resistance again and again—even when these tactics do not result in the desired outcome. In the following story about Frank and Ms. Winston, Maag (1997) illustrates this point:

> It just wasn't fair, thought Frank, as he leaned up against the wall of the school scraping the mud off his shoes. It wasn't actually mud, but a combination of clay and sand from the infield of the school baseball diamond. And this stuff was sticky. The bottom of his shoes looked like a stack of pancakes that had been covered with too much syrup and then ignored. He had already broken three sticks trying to remove the stuff and was now using his last pencil which, he figured, was only good for about two scrapes. That would be another problem: When he returned to class Ms. Winston would give him the standard lecture of coming prepared with enough pencils. "I'm sick of her telling me what to do," Frank said aloud to no one in particular.
>
> It was the first day that had been warm enough to go outside for recess. The bright sun had melted the last of the snow and although the ground was soaking wet, that didn't stop the children from playing games like four-square. It seemed to Frank like recess just started when the bell rang signaling its end. Ms. Winston, his fifth-grade teacher, had recess duty this day. She spoke the routine every child knew by heart: "Line up next to the wall, no talking, hands to self, and no bouncing the balls." It was this last rule with which Frank and the other kids had fun. Billy was standing in front of Frank holding one of the balls used to play four-square. Suddenly Frank reached over and swatted the ball out of Billy's hand. But he had not counted on Ms. Winston turning around to face him at that very moment. A couple of kids started laughing as the ball rolled toward them. One of the kids, Randy Johnson, took this opportunity to kick the ball as hard as he could. It went flying right into the middle of the soaking wet baseball diamond. "Frank, go pick up that ball," Ms. Winston said sternly.

"But I didn't kick it over there," whined Frank. "It's not fair that I should have to walk on that muddy baseball diamond to get a ball I didn't kick over there." From the expression on Ms. Winston's face—a cross between marine drill sergeant and pitbull—Frank knew the discussion was over. Yet he couldn't resist making one more plea. "I'm going to get my shoes really muddy and you wouldn't want me to track mud in the classroom? Why don't we have the janitor get the ball?" Rather than responding, Ms. Winston turned away from Frank and instructed the children to go inside.

Frank had retrieved the ball and was now scraping the mud off his shoes. "Snap," went his last pencil as a clog of mud resembling a miniature frisbee went flying off his shoe. He knew Ms. Winston would still be angry at him as he shuffled his feet one last time on the concrete before entering the building. "Fine," he thought, "let her be angry. I don't care. She's not going to tell me what to do." When Frank entered Ms. Winston's room he was still determined not to let her tell him what to do again.

"Please get your reading book off the shelf, take it back to your desk, and open it to page 27," said Ms. Winston when Frank entered the room. Frank absentmindedly picked up his reading book from the shelf and started walking back to his desk. Then he thought how Ms. Winston was again trying to tell him what to do. He was fed up with teachers telling him what he could and couldn't do. He turned back toward Ms. Winston, dropped the book on the floor and glared at her challengingly.

Ms. Winston calmly said, "Frank, please pick up your book and take a seat."

"No, I won't pick up my book. And I'm not going to sit in my chair either. You can't make me—nobody can make me!"

At this point, Frank could be considered "oppositional," and Ms. Winston must deal with his resistance. She cannot back down because her authority has been challenged. Therefore, to maintain discipline and the respect of the other students, Ms. Winston must make Frank pick up the book and sit in his chair or suffer the consequences. Ms. Winston responded to Frank's resistance by saying, "Frank, if you don't pick up the book right now, you'll be eating lunch by yourself in the classroom today." Frank just stood there, his bottom lip stuck out like the perch on a bird house, his silence communicating his answer. "Fine," said Ms. Winston. "You can just go down to the principal's office right now and she can give your mother a call" (pp. 229-231).

The situation depicted in the story of Frank and Ms. Winston is a common one—repeated in many classrooms every day. Let's take a closer look at this story. Who is being resistant—Frank or his teacher? Frank's behavior is rational and purposeful, given the situation as he interpreted it. Ms. Winston on the other hand used the typical, unimaginative ways of responding and, so, was unable to obtain the desired behavior from Frank. Furthermore, her responses gave Frank exactly what he desired—power and control.

Frank's behavior served a function. It helped him regain the power and control Ms. Winston had taken away. Throwing the book on the floor was the least important aspect of Frank's interaction with Ms. Winston. He could have just as easily made animal noises, ran around the classroom, or been otherwise disruptive. His motivation was to get Ms. Winston to tell him what to do, so that he could refuse her request and take back the personal power and control he had lost. Ms. Winston did not get what she desired—compliance. Yet, she will most likely continue to use this same approach again when faced with resistance. (Power and control are further elaborated on in Part IV.)

We have to stop and ask ourselves why we spend large amounts of time doing the same thing over and over in an attempt to get students to be more cooperative and to follow our instructions when it doesn't work. In order to break this ineffective pattern, we need to step out of our current paradigm that resistance originates with students. Instead, we need to embrace a new paradigm—that it is *our* behavior that creates resistance. In other words, resistance is the result of what we communicate to our students. If we never asked our students to do anything, they would never be resistant! Of course, we cannot manage resistance by letting students do whatever they want. But we can take a new approach. By shifting our views of, and our responses to, student behaviors, we can manage resistance more effectively. This perspective is based largely on the work and teachings of Milton H. Erickson, M.D.

The Remarkable Milton H. Erickson, M.D.

Rossi, Ryan, and Sharp (1983) begin their discussion of Erickson with the following question: "How can we draw a picture of the life of that wily American farm boy who had enough mischievousness to outfox tragic personal illness and become a genius in healing and hypnosis?" (p. 1). The best place to start is his childhood.

"Each person is a unique individual. Hence, psychotherapy should be formulated to meet the uniqueness of the individual's needs, rather than tailoring the person to fit the Procrustean bed of a hypothetical theory of human behavior."

-Milton H. Erickson, M.D.

Milton Erickson was raised on a small farm in Wisconsin. He was color-blind, tone-deaf, and dyslexic. These afflictions became an asset for Erickson:

So much is communicated by the way a person speaks.... My tone-deafness has forced me to pay attention to inflections in the voice. This means I'm less distracted by the content of what people say. Many patterns of behavior are reflected in the way a person says something rather than in what he says (Haley, 1993, p. 3).

Erickson began to use techniques in his childhood that he would later refine. For example, Erickson (1975) recounted that he used the double bind, or paradoxical intervention (at the time the term had not yet been coined):

One winter day, with the weather below zero, my father led a calf out of the barn to the water trough. After the calf had satisfied its thirst, they turned back to the barn, but at the doorway the calf stubbornly braced its feet, and despite my father's desperate pulling on the halter, he could not budge the animal. I was outside playing in the snow and, observing the impasse, began laughing heartily. My father challenged me to pull the calf into the barn. Recognizing *the situation as one of unreasoning stubborn resistance on the part of the calf, I decided to let the calf have full opportunity to resist since that was what it apparently wished to do. Accordingly I presented the calf with a double bind by seizing it by the tail and pulling it away from the barn, while my father continued to pull it inward. The calf promptly chose to resist the weaker of the two forces and dragged me into the barn (p. 412).*

Perhaps the most significant experience of Erickson's young life was when he was stricken with polio at the age of 17. He overheard three physicians tell his parents that he would be dead by morning. Erickson did not die that night. Awakening after three days, Erickson found himself paralyzed except for being able to see and hear, move his eyes, and speak with great difficulty. He spent much of his time tied into a rocking chair with a hole in the seat that functioned as a primitive commode. One day, Erickson sat and wished to be closer to the window. He noticed that his chair began rocking slightly. In this simple way, Erickson discovered the basic ideomotor principle of hypnosis discussed by Bernheim: the idea of movement can lead to the automatic body movement. With this discovery, Erickson began to exercise his sense memories. He would remember what it felt like to pick up a spoon, grasp a pitchfork, and climb a tree. One day Erickson's fingers began to twitch in tiny uncoordinated ways. Additional exercises activated more sense memories, restimulating his sensory-motor coordination. He was able to walk on crutches within a year.

Eventually Erickson went to college. He learned hypnosis and attended medical school, completing his training at the Colorado Psychopathic Hospital. He went on to become chief psychiatrist at the Worcester State Hospital, then became the director of psychiatric research and training at Wayne County General Hospital and Infirmary in Eloise, Michigan. In 1948, Erickson accepted a position as clinical director at the Arizona State Hospital in Phoenix, Arizona. A year later, he began a private practice.

Throughout his career, Erickson placed great emphasis on the importance of carefully observing clients. His observational skills, developed as a result of his acute awareness during paralysis, his unorthodox approaches, and his great success with clients, made him much sought after. Today Erickson's techniques are used in a wide variety of healing areas. The techniques most relevant to working with resistance in the classroom are collected for the first time in this book.

Note. Illustration and quote from *Ericksonian Psychotherapy* (p. viii). Edited by Zeig, J.K., 1998. New York: Brunner/Mazel. Illustration by Barry Shepard. Reprinted with permission.

Chapter 2
_____

Understanding Resistance

Just the word "resistance" is enough to make most educators shudder. Arguing, scapegoating, fighting, swearing, passivity, and avoidance, are a few of the common occurrences of resistance we have to contend with. We describe resistance as being noncompliant, oppositional, contrary, obstinate, bullheaded, and stubborn. Unfortunately, the behaviors and words we use to describe resistance fail to take into account the purposes behind them. In the following sections, three viewpoints for understanding resistance are presented. These three viewpoints form the basis for most of the interventions described in this book.

What Is Resistance?

Some definitions of resistance begin by defining compliance. Compliance is sometimes conceptualized as obedience to our directives and prohibitions, cooperation with requests, or the willingness to accept suggestions in teaching situations. Noncompliance, then, involves disobedience to directives, uncooperativeness with requests, and unwillingness to accept suggestions. Students may be noncompliant by refusing to comply, refusing to respond, or engaging in unrequested behaviors.

In this book, the term resistance carries a more functional connotation: **resistance is created when we fail to determine the world view from which a student operates and fail to modify our behavior accordingly.** In the story of Frank and Ms. Winston (Chapter 1), Ms. Winston failed to communicate effectively with Frank. The story illustrates how resistance originates solely from our behavior.

Several years ago while conducting a workshop, I placed a transparency of *Figure 1-3* on the overhead projector. Joseph, an extremely intelligent clinical psychologist who was sitting in the back of the room, vehemently shook his head back and forth indicating his disagreement. This is the ensuing dialogue:

> "So, Joseph, I gather that you disagree with my statement."
>
> "Yes," replied Joseph, "I believe resistance results from the interaction between two or more persons' behaviors." I proceeded by asking Joseph some questions: "Joseph, you disagree with me? Do we have opposing

Insanity: Doing the same thing the same way and expecting different results.

positions? Are our viewpoints contrary to each other? Is there resistance to accepting the other's definition?"

Joseph nodded in the affirmative to each question. "You just made my point!" I said.

Joseph had a puzzled look, so I continued by asking him several more questions: "What if I had placed a transparency on the overhead projector that said 'Resistance results from the interaction of two or more persons' behaviors?'"

Joseph said we would be in agreement.

"So, in that case, we would not have opposing positions? Our viewpoints would not be contrary? You would not be resistant to my assertion?"

This time, Joseph understood my point—it was I that had the power to either create or eliminate his resistance. If I made statements with which Joseph agreed, then there was no resistance. If I made

statements with which Joseph disagreed, then resistance was created.

The conceptualization of resistance illustrated by our dialogue conveys good news and bad news. The good news is that the only person's behavior over which we have total control is our own. Therefore, resistance can be eliminated by changing our behaviors, rather than lamenting the intractability of students' behaviors. The bad news is that changing our behaviors is difficult—especially when students present us with their own challenging behaviors. As we proceed, keep in mind that challenging behaviors are displayed by students for whom traditional behavior management techniques have failed.

Three Viewpoints on Resistance

Three different viewpoints can help us better understand the nature of resistance. First, we will examine Freud's viewpoint. Freud was probably the first to describe resistance within a psychotherapeutic framework. The second viewpoint we will discuss is derived from the family therapy literature. The third viewpoint, stemming from the behavioral literature, serves as a key for understanding how to effectively manage resistance by analyzing the context of behavior and the function a behavior serves.

The Freudian View

Sigmund Freud has been lavishly praised and fiercely chastised for his theories. Both glorified and denounced as a person, he is regarded as a

Figure 1-3
Resistance originates solely from your behavior!

great scientist, a cult leader, and a fraud. Regardless of the adulation and criticism Freud has received, few would deny the incredible impact his ideas have had on Western culture. Freud's psychodynamic theory has permeated our everyday lives. Just think of how many phrases we use that he coined—phrases such as "egocentric," "slip of the tongue," and "anal retentive."

Although many aspects of Freud's theory either have not withstood the test of empirical study or have few practical implications, his conceptualization of resistance is quite illuminating. Freud used the term "resistance" to describe why many of his patients failed to participate in therapy despite their request for help. Why would a person be motivated to seek out therapy but then resist a therapist's help? Freud speculated that resistance served an adaptive function: It maintained internal equilibrium and helped the person avoid consciously experiencing emotional conflict. If a client was to fully comply with therapy, he would be exposing himself to the anxiety associated with the problem that prompted the plea for help, thus risking feeling worse—at least initially. By being resistant to therapy, the client keeps the anxiety at an unconscious level, which, in the short run, is less emotionally painful than confronting it directly.

The Family Systems View

The family systems viewpoint focuses on relationships rather than viewing an individual's problems in isolation. The family process is holistic, or systemic, and focuses on the context that provides

meaning to behavior. School therapists who utilize this model recognize that although the presenting problem may be centered on a student, it may be maintained by behaviors of other members of the classroom (e.g., peers and teachers). The problem behavior affects the behavior of other students and teachers. For example, there was a teenage boy who frequently stayed out past his curfew. He was caught shoplifting, twice ran away from home, and even started fires in his backyard. The parents were having marital difficulties that were apparent to the boy by their intense arguments. His delinquent behaviors successfully terminated the parents' arguing because they "pulled together" to deal with their son. Knowing his parents had been arguing that day, the son stayed out past his curfew. His parents subsequently worked in a concerted effort to determine his whereabouts. The boy would be extremely resistant to changing his behavior as long as he believed his parents were having marital difficulties.

The family systems viewpoint of resistance is similar to Freud's, but without the psychodynamic undertones. From this perspective, students choose to cling to the way things are, rather than expose themselves to uncertainty. For example, some students complain of not having enough friends, wanting more money, or being bored, yet they are resistant to suggestions to join a club, apply for a job, or develop a hobby. The reason has to do with risk—all of the suggestions expose the student to the potential risk of rejection or

People don't enter therapy to cure their neuroses, but rather to perfect them.

failure. The pain implied is more severe than the pain of remaining the same.

Because of the risk involved in change, we all repeat certain behaviors even though they are ineffective. We try to maintain homeostasis—a term family therapists use to describe the desire for consistency in our lives. Consistency breeds predictability. Predictability reduces anxiety and engenders feelings of comfort and self-assurance. Students repeatedly engage in inappropriate behaviors, and we, in turn, respond in predictable and often ineffective ways.

Behavioral View

A key concept in managing resistance is context. Behavior does not occur in a random or unorganized fashion. We behave purposely, and our behavior retains its meaning as a function of the context—the situation or circumstances in a particular environment: lifeguards have more meaning by the side of a pool than on a ski slope; reading a book has more meaning in a library than it does in a game of soccer. Very few behaviors could be universally considered inappropriate. Running and yelling provides an obvious example. In the context of a math lesson, running and yelling is inappropriate. In the context of a basketball game, this behavior would be acceptable, or perhaps even valued. A more dramatic example involves cutting someone's throat with a knife—clearly a behavior most of us would consider aberrant, especially within the context of a mugging or robbery. However, this behavior would be quite appropriate if someone was performing an emergency tracheotomy on a person choking. Almost all behaviors are appropriate in a certain context or frame of reference.

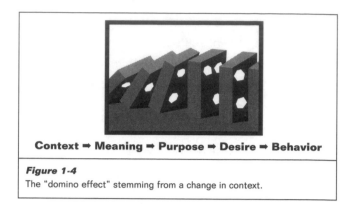

Context ➡ Meaning ➡ Purpose ➡ Desire ➡ Behavior

Figure 1-4
The "domino effect" stemming from a change in context.

Contextual Manipulation

Unfortunately, most of the time we focus solely on the appearance of a behavior and fail to examine its context—especially when the behavior is considered highly inappropriate. A good example of this is when a second-grader mistakenly brought her mother's lunch to school. In the sack was a paring knife to cut an apple. The girl was summarily expelled because the school had a "zero tolerance" policy for students carrying weapons. The girl did not have a history of behavior problems at school, nor did her behavior constitute a threat to herself or others. Nevertheless, school officials ignored the context surrounding this behavior. The community backlash at the school's insensitivity, rigidity, and lack of "common sense" resulted in the administration readmitting the student several days later.

The implication of context for managing resistance is deceptively simple. When we manipulate the context surrounding a behavior, a "domino effect" is created, depicted in *Figure 1-4*, that results in a change in behavior. For example, whenever a teacher instructed her class to line up for recess, one of her students would swear. The **context**, or situation, was being told to line up for recess. The **meaning** the student attached to the request was that the teacher was trying to force him to do something he didn't want to do.

The **purpose** of the student's swearing was to obtain power and control ("she can't make me do what I don't want to do"). The reinforcing value of obtaining power and control by getting a reaction, even a negative one, fueled the student's desire to continue engaging in the inappropriate behavior.

A different picture emerged when the teacher changed the context surrounding the inappropriate behavior. The next time the student began swearing, the teacher nonchalantly told the student that he was not being creative in his swearing. She enthusiastically and sincerely suggested that he begin swearing before she told the class to line up. The boy, who began in earnest because this request was congruent with what he wanted to do, quickly lost interest and quietly lined up for recess. The teacher's instruction to swear changed the context in several ways. First, when the student began swearing as requested, he was no longer being resistant but rather compliant. Second, in order to continue being resistant, he would have to stop swearing. Third, the teacher's attitude was that she would be pleased rather than angry if the student engaged in the misbehavior. By changing the context and meaning of swearing in these three ways, the purpose of obtaining power and control was altered, the desire ceased, and the behavior was eliminated.

There are endless ways in which we can manipulate context in order to obtain a desired result. Parents often sit between siblings at a movie theater to reduce misbehavior; teachers move disruptive students to a different part of the room or tell the student who is shooting paper balls at the trash can to stay after school and repeatedly throw paper in the can. Most context manipulation techniques involve having a student engage in the misbehavior—assuming that the behavior is not dangerous to self or others—but to do it over and over again or at a different time or location.

The word **manipulation** often has a negative connotation for those of us who work with students with challenging behaviors. However, manipulation need not be viewed as something devious. The very process of teaching is manipulative. Teachers manipulate materials, curricula, and instructional techniques. In fact, every interaction we have can be considered a manipulation, since the goal is usually to elicit a response. Learning to manipulate effectively, relevantly, and constructively will have a profoundly positive impact on managing resistance. Following is an example that is particularly illustrative of contextual manipulation.

Over three decades ago, Ayllon (1963) treated a hospitalized psychiatric patient who hoarded and stored large numbers of towels in her room. The treatment consisted of having the nurses go into the patient's room every day and hand her an increasing number of towels. After accumulating more than 600 towels, the patient began taking a few out of her room. At that point, no more towels were handed to her. Over the course of a year, the average number of towels in her room decreased to one to five per week as compared with 13 to 29 before the intervention.

Unfortunately, Ayllon's intervention lacked an essential component that must be present with every context manipulation technique for managing resistance: determining the function an inappropriate behavior serves and then teaching and reinforcing a replacement behavior—an appropriate behavior that serves the same function as the inappropriate behavior. All behaviors—those deemed unacceptable as well as acceptable—are purposeful and serve a function. Neel and Cessna (1993) used the term **behavioral intent** to describe the relation between the behavior exhibited by a child and the outcome he or she desired. When a child acts, even with inappropriate behaviors, he or she does so to achieve a result. The desired result, or outcome, can be viewed as the intent or function of the behavior. In turn, the intent of the behavior will impact the form (i.e., the appearance or topography) of the behavior. It

is entirely possible for the function of a behavior to be appropriate while the form of the behavior is inappropriate.

There are two ways the importance of behavioral intent can be illustrated using Ayllon's study. First, the purpose of hoarding towels needed to be identified. It is possible that the patient hoarded to obtain power and control, attention, or both. Therefore, she would have to be taught and reinforced for using a replacement behavior. Perhaps the patient could have worked collaboratively with the staff to decide on her daily schedule and provide them with input on when she was ready for a home pass. These replacement behaviors may have provided a way for the patient to achieve power and control over her treatment. (Psychiatric hospitals of the early 1960s typically did not promote and reinforce patient autonomy and independent thinking.) If hoarding was performed to obtain attention, then the patient may have been taught to ask for assistance or to request that a staff member talk with her at appropriate times. Without teaching a replacement behavior and reinforcing it, the result would be that the patient would display other inappropriate behaviors to obtain the desired outcomes.

The second way the Ayllon study illustrates the importance of behavioral intent is the role of the nurses. When handing the patient increasing amounts of towels, it would have been important for the nurses to display an attitude of being pleased that the patient now had an opportunity to become even better at hoarding. In this way, the nurses would eliminate any power and control value the patient may have been seeking by seeing them angry and frustrated at her hoarding.

These two considerations are elaborated on throughout this book, particularly in Chapter 7.

Chapter 3

The Nature of Rapport

Manipulating context and teaching replacement behaviors are much easier when we have first established rapport. Rapport can be conceptualized as the opposite of resistance. The nature of rapport warrants elaboration because it is essential for obtaining a desired outcome.

Rapport is typically associated with the Carl Rogers person-centered counseling approach (Rogers, 1951). This approach focuses on providing individuals with genuine unconditional positive regard, empathy, and honesty as a way to promote self-acceptance and self-responsibility. Rapport is neither the ability to be sympathetic nor the outcome of being liked by a student. Sympathy and pleasant interactions are often erroneously taken as evidence of rapport. **Rapport** is our ability to symmetrically respond to another person's viewpoint or model of the world. Rapport is created when a student accepts our behaviors as an accurate representation of his or her ongoing experience. This acceptance increases the likelihood that the student will be compliant with our directions.

It is not easy to determine how students construct meaning from the world—no two people understand the same experience the same way. Each person has unique interpretations and has organized those interpretations into an equally unique set of

judgments about the nature of the world. Individuals create a unique set of rules by which to live relative to the context in which his or her view is operating (Gordon & Meyers-Anderson, 1981).

Students' personal views about the world and themselves are not usually explicitly stated—they are covert. It is not possible for us to really know how they think. However, students' beliefs are implicit in their verbal and nonverbal behaviors. For example, when a student asks, "When do you want the homework turned in?" we can infer that she believes it is important to consult the teacher, that she believes the teacher has useful information about her, and that she believes there is an optimum time to hand in the assignment. When a student communicates to us, the content of that communication is based on, and indicative of, certain beliefs held within that student's model of the world. It is more beneficial to demonstrate that we understand and accept the student's

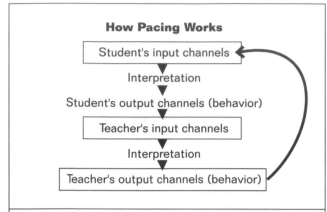

Figure 1-5
Pacing, and consequently rapport, occurs when the teacher's output behavior is congruent with the student's output behavior.
Note. From *Patterns of the hypnotic techniques of Milton H. Erickson, M.D.: Vol.1* (p.17), by Bandler, R. and Grinder, J., 1975, Capitola, CA: Meta Publications (831) 464-0254. Reprinted with permission.

model of the world as being valid than it is to try to directly alter a student's beliefs.

In order to enter a student's frame of reference, we need to pace his or her ongoing verbal and non-verbal behaviors. **Pacing**, illustrated in *Figure 1-5*, is the process of carefully observing a student's verbal and nonverbal behavior and then reflecting back to him or her what is observed (Bandler and Grinder, 1975). It is a process whereby we respond by matching the student's verbal and nonverbal behaviors in order to create rapport. Pacing makes it easier to obtain a desired outcome. In *Figure 1-5* the student takes in information from the five senses—visual, auditory, tactile, auditory, and gustatory (input channels). This information is then organized into schema and connected to past experiences that seem relevant. The student then interprets the information in a way that guides his or her behavior (output channels). The teacher then goes through the same process of taking in the student's behavior through his or her input channels, interpreting it, and outputting a behavior based on the interpretation.

Pacing, and consequently rapport, occurs when the teacher's output behavior matches the student's output behavior. For example, when a student faces you with her hands folded across her chest and says "You can't make me," you have two ways to respond. An incongruent response would be "You will do as I tell you or suffer the consequences." This response creates resistance because it does not match the student's world view of being oppositional as a way to gain power and control. The student will simply ignore your requests and threats. On the other hand, rapport is created if you respond by saying "You are right. I can't make you." This response would be congruent with the student's behavior. It results in compliance. In order for the student to maintain a resistant frame of mind, he or she would have to respond by saying "Oh, yes you *can* make me!" This unlikely response would be necessary for the student to do the opposite of what you said. On the other hand, if the student says, "You're right, you can't make me," you have created rapport. Both of your output behaviors are congruent. It then becomes easier to move the student in the direction of a desired outcome.

Students will be less resistant to engaging in requested behaviors when we pace the content of their models of the world. Pacing demonstrates that we respect, share, and preserve their models. In this story, related by Rosen (1982), Erickson unknowingly establishes rapport by feeding back a frame of reference:

> *One summer I sold books to pay my way through college. I walked into a farmyard about five o'clock, interviewed the farmer about buying books, and he said, "Young fellow, I don't read anything. I don't need to read anything. I'm just interested in my hogs."*

"While you're busy feeding the hogs, do you mind if I stand and talk to you?" I asked.

He said, "No, talk away, young fellow, it won't do you a bit of good. I'm not going to pay attention to you; I am busy feeding the hogs."

And so I talked about my books. Being a farm boy, I thoughtlessly picked up a pair of shingles lying on the ground and started scratching the hogs' backs as I was talking. The farmer looked over, stopped, and said, "Anybody that knows how to scratch a hog's back, the way hogs like it, is somebody I want to know. How about having supper with me tonight and you can sleep overnight with no charge and I will buy your books. You like hogs. You know how to scratch 'em the way they liked to be scratched" (p. 59).

This story is not an illustration of how to sell books or manipulate people. It demonstrates that through his behavior, Erickson was genuinely able to relate to this farmer. The behavior of scratching the hogs' backs was unconscious and doubtlessly related to the fact that Erickson grew up on a farm. Nevertheless, he was able to establish rapport and achieve his purpose by joining the farmer in his frame of reference.

By pacing a student's verbal and nonverbal behaviors, we create rapport, increasing the likelihood of a desired outcome. Erickson was an expert at pacing because he could make minute visual and auditory distinctions. (He acquired this skill when an attack of polio left him immobile, with little to do but observe the environment. He later recovered.) When working with a client, Erickson adopted the client's tonality, syntax, and tempo of speech. He also matched the client's body position, breathing rate, and ges-

tures. Matching created a congruence between Erickson and his client. Erickson's sophisticated use of pacing even included using a different body part or function to pace a client's behavior. For example, Erickson might match the tempo of his voice to a client's breathing rate by watching the client's chest expand and contract.

Clients were rarely aware of the complex way in which Erickson was pacing them. Bandler and Grinder (1975) suggested that the client's lack of awareness was an essential component of Erickson's ability to induce a rapid and effective hypnotic trance. While addressing a group of professionals in Mexico City in 1959, Erickson quite amazingly hypnotized a woman who could neither speak nor understand English, using only

gestures and body movement. This approach became known as the "pantomime technique."

Erickson's use of pacing to induce trance can also work in developing rapport. Three pacing techniques follow: matching predicates, postural congruence, and cross-over mirroring.

Matching Predicates

One way to pace the verbal content of a student's communication is to match the characteristic use of predicates—words that imply specific action and relations, i.e., verbs and their modifiers. Most people typically rely on one or two sensory modalities (visual, auditory, kinesthetic, tactile) to communicate our experiences. For example, a student who says, "I know that I should have had a better *grasp* of the material, but I ran into so many *stumbling blocks*," has represented this situation through the tactile and kinesthetic modalities. A student who says, "When everything was *clear* to me, I could *picture* the whole situation, and *see* the answers," is operating out of the visual modality. If a student says, "It's hard for me to *hear* what you're *telling* me, and it just didn't *sound* right," he or she is using the auditory modality. If we match our own predicates to those our students use most often, the consistent result is that the students experience someone who literally "speaks their language." They experience that we understand them and are understandable, and are therefore trustworthy (Gordon & Meyers-Anderson, 1981). Rapport is established. It is then easier to move a student in the direction of a desired outcome.

Postural Congruence

Another way to establish rapport is to pace students' analogical behaviors. **Analogical behav-**

iors refers to breathing rates, body postures, muscle tensions, facial expressions, gross body movements, voice tonalities, and intonation patterns. The effect of this type of mirroring, or **postural congruence**, is that our behavior becomes closely identified with that of the students. We become an unconscious, accurate source of feedback as to what the student is doing. At the most fundamental level, we directly copy some, or all, of the analogical behavior of the student. If a student talks with a high-pitched voice and is fidgety, we match that behavior by raising our own tonality and by squirming in our chair. In order for postural congruence to be effective, we must develop extremely astute observation skills and engage in the analogical behavior subtly, so as not to draw the student's attention to this process or embarrass him or her in front of classmates. Even if a student does observe that we are copying his or her behavior, the result is often paradoxical: the student stops engaging in the inappropriate behavior in order to comment on our copying.

Cross-Over Mirroring

A more sophisticated form of postural congruence is called cross-over mirroring. In cross-over mirroring, we copy the analogical behavior using a part of the body, or an output system, that is different from that being used by the student. For example, the nervous tapping of a student's foot can be mirrored by subtly bobbing your head or by raising the pitch of your voice in rhythm to the tapping. The possibilities for cross-over mirroring are limitless. The advantage is that students are less likely to recognize our actions as an attempt to copy their behaviors.

PART II

From Child to Context

Chapter 4

Two Models for Working with Resistance

We are often quick to point to students as the source of resistance. This focus seemingly makes sense because many definitions of resistance focus on disobedience to directives, uncooperativeness with requests, or an unwillingness to accept suggestions. Students who actively refuse to follow directions, provide no response, or engage in inappropriate behaviors represent a major concern and challenge for us. In fact, many educators view these behaviors as characteristic of Oppositional Defiant Disorder—a pattern of negativistic, hostile, and defiant behavior which includes at least four of the eight behaviors appearing in *Table 2-1*.

The Medical-Disease Model of Resistance

Oppositional Defiant Disorder is based on the medical-disease model. In this model, clusters of noncompliant behaviors can exist within students just as physical diseases can. These clusters are discrete and identifiable. The medical-disease model has received widespread approval and is used almost exclusively throughout psychiatry. However, this model fails to take into account that behavior problems are socially negotiated and socially defined.

Social norms and standards vary across contexts and times. Imagine watching the 1960s television

sitcom *The Andy Griffith Show*. Think of the situations Opie found himself in and the behaviors he exhibited. Now think about the three kids on the 1990s sitcom *Roseanne* and the behaviors they exhibited. What if we juxtaposed the behaviors of the *Roseanne* kids with Opie's behavior? Wouldn't Opie's behaviors look bizarre and aberrant? The standards and norms for children's appropriate behaviors in the early 1960s are far different than the standards of the 1990s. If Opie had behaved like the children on *Roseanne*, he probably would have been referred to a psychiatrist and, most likely, diagnosed as having a behavior disorder. The irony is that Opie's problems would have been nothing more than a case of bad timing—

Has the student demonstrated four or more of these behaviors in a six-month period?

❏ 1. Often loses temper

❏ 2. Often argues with adults

❏ 3. Often actively defies or refuses to comply with adults' requests or rules

❏ 4. Often deliberately annoys people

❏ 5. Often blames others for his or her mistakes or misbehaviors

❏ 6. Is often touchy or easily annoyed by others

❏ 7. Is often angry and resentful

❏ 8. Is often spiteful or vindictive

Table 2-1
The criteria used to determine whether a student is displaying Oppositional Defiant Disorder.

being three decades ahead of the accepted societal standards for children's behaviors of the 1990s.

Teachers also have their own personal standards of what they consider abnormal behavior, based on their social, cultural, ethical, and religious backgrounds. Therefore, "noncompliant" behaviors may reflect the standards or the tolerance level of a teacher more accurately than any deviance exhibited by students. Attention Deficit Hyperactivity Disorder (ADHD) provides a telling example of this point. ADHD is characterized by inattention, impulsivity, and hyperactivity. The last characteristic, hyperactivity, refers to the level of a child's motor movement. This trait is probably evenly distributed throughout the population: most people have some average level of motor movement; some have very high motor movement (hyperactivity); and others have very low motor movement (hypoactivity).

Teachers have distinct tolerance levels concerning hyperactivity.

Some teachers tolerate more motor movement than other teachers. Teacher tolerance levels can either facilitate or inhibit the use of effective behavior management techniques.

There are two pairs of traits depicted in *Figure 2-1*: motor movement and teacher tolerance. Student 1's degree of motor movement falls between Line D and Line E. This level of motor movement may be associated with hyperactivity. However, the other trait—teacher tolerance—also plays a part. Teacher 2 can tolerate extreme displays of hyperactive behavior. On the other hand, Teacher 1's tolerance level is extremely low. Teacher 1 is not likely to put up with many displays of inappropriate behavior. If most of Teacher 1's students display motor movements that fall between A and C, does Student 2's motor movement constitute a problem? This scenario illustrates that inappropriate behaviors involve the tolerance levels, standards, values, and behaviors of teachers. Here is a telling example of this point:

> An 8-year-old boy was referred to a therapist to treat his hyperactivity. The boy

appeared as if he was not listening because of his high motor movement—even though he comprehended most of what was told to him. The therapist met with the boy's third-grade teacher. She came up with an innovative plan. She would give the boy three desks: two in each front corner of the room and one in the back middle of the room. The boy was told that he could move from one desk to another whenever he felt the urge, as long as he did not disrupt other students. The boy was also reinforced for moving quietly. This intervention was successful. The boy's hyperactivity was not a problem in this class and he was able to learn and be productive. The following year however, his fourth-grade teacher refused to make this three-desk accommodation. She felt that if she gave him three desks, then every student would want three desks. As a result, this teacher ended up calling the mother about once a week because the boy's hyperactivity created disturbances in the class.

This story further demonstrates the essential role teachers play in managing resistance. It's not the student, but the teacher who creates success or failure for the student.

The Can't or Won't Model of Resistance

An alternative to viewing noncompliant behaviors as disorders, developed by Howell and Nolet (2000), appears in *Figure 2-2*. Using this model, we can examine a student's resistant behavior in

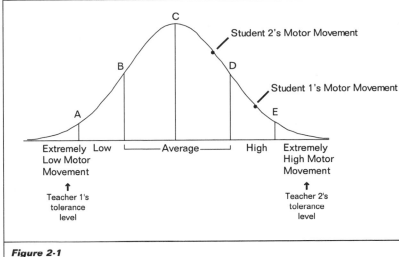

Figure 2-1
Normal curve depicting interaction between student behavior and teacher tolerance levels.

relation to two general categories: can't versus can. If a student appears resistant, there are two possible reasons. First, he or she may lack the requisite skills necessary to comply with the request (Type 1 Prerequisites: Skills). For example, a teacher may tell a student to "stop irritating" her neighbor. However, the student may not know what "irritate" means specifically or may not know how to appropriately obtain attention from her peer. She is unable to comply with the teacher's request and so appears resistant.

The second reason the student may appear resistant is that some aspect of the environment may be reinforcing the behavior (Type 1 Prerequisites: Environment). For example, if she is receiving a lot of attention from the peer for "being irritating," she may continue to engage in the undesirable behavior—despite the teacher's direction.

If a student *can* perform the requested behavior (i.e., all the Type 1 Prerequisites have been met) but still resists, there may be a variety of reasons (Type 2 Prerequisites). The student's beliefs about a situation may interfere with performing the desired behavior. For example, when a student gets into a playground fight we often require him

> *When a child purposely performs a behavior to irritate us, he is reacting to us as much as we are reacting to him.*

to apologize to the offended classmate. However, he may be quite resistant to making an apology—not because he lacks the skills for apologizing, but because he believes his peers will think he is weak. The student's belief creates resistance.

Another reason why a student *won't* perform a requested behavior is that he or she selected an inappropriate strategy. Strategies help us analyze a situation, select a behavior to perform based on our analysis, and evaluate the possible consequences. Sometimes we fail to evaluate correctly. For example, a student responds to a peer who is teasing by hitting her. As a result, the student receives in-school suspension for two days. The next time she is teased, the student might hit again. Because she fails to evaluate the consequences, or perhaps because she used this tactic

successfully before—without consequences—the student selects this strategy.

It is important to understand that when students won't perform the appropriate behavior, it means they have selected, from among a variety of behaviors, the wrong behavior—one that makes them appear resistant or oppositional. They may not consciously intend to irritate us. When students *do* purposely perform a behavior to irritate us, they are reacting to us as much as we are reacting to them. In this instance, resistance results from our inability to modify our behavior to obtain student compliance.

Selecting an inappropriate behavior is not the same thing as *deciding* to behave inappropriately. Students automatically select inappropriate behaviors without giving conscious thought to the consequences. These automatic behaviors have become habitual through repeated use and are unconscious.

The remainder of Part II is devoted to describing techniques for managing resistance that roughly correspond to the Type 1 and Type 2 Prerequisites appearing in *Figure 2-2*. Students who lack the necessary skills represent a Type 1 Prerequisite-skill deficit. (The other Type 1 Prerequisite, environmental factors, is addressed separately in Part III.)

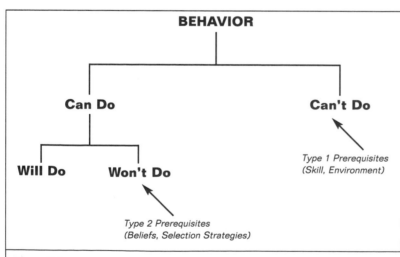

Figure 2-2
Model for understanding resistance based on whether a student doesn't know how to perform a behavior or selects an inappropriate behavior. *Note.* Adapted from *Curriculum-based evaluation teaching and decision making*, 3rd edition, by Howell, K.W. and Nolet, V. © 2000. Reprinted with permission of Wadsworth, an imprint of Wadsworth Group, a division of Thomson Learning. Fax (800) 730-2215.

Pessimistic expectations or anxious thoughts pertain to **beliefs** (a Type 2 Prerequisite). Although the techniques that follow focus on student factors, implementing the strategies effectively nevertheless involves changing our behavior and mindset toward oppositional and noncompliant behavior.

All techniques in this book can be used with students of all ages and grades. Of course, you will need to modify them based on each individual student's developmental, cognitive, social, and emotional level.

Chapter 5

Helping Students Who Lack the Necessary Skills
(a Type 1 Prerequisite)

There are few situations as likely to trigger noncompliance as requiring students to perform a task for which they lack the necessary skills. This situation frequently occurs when students are required to engage in independent seatwork. Years of teacher effectiveness research has provided important findings related to independent seatwork. First, research indicates that there are three levels of skill proficiency students can demonstrate (Mastropieri and Scruggs, 1994):

1. **Accuracy** (doing a task correctly)

2. **Fluency** (doing a task correctly and quickly)

3. **Automaticity** (doing a task accurately, at a high rate, within a relevant context).

An automatic level of proficiency is often required for students to succeed at independent practice.

The second point made in the research is that students with learning difficulties benefit most from guided practice (either teacher-led, small-group questions and answers or immediate teacher monitoring of written student responses) prior to engaging in independent practice. Despite this research, many teachers go directly from presentation of material to independent practice.

The third point made in the research is that most students should achieve 85–95 percent accuracy at a task *under teacher guidance* before moving on to independent practice.

Many behavior problems occur when we ask students to perform tasks for which they have not reached sufficient accuracy, fluency, or automaticity. Many times we only teach to the accuracy level. Once students give correct responses, we move on to new content. Many times we don't assess a student's fluency (accuracy and speed), yet fluency is a prerequisite for doing work independently. For example, a teacher may have just delivered a math lesson on division. She then gives her students a worksheet containing 15 division problems to complete at their desks by the end of the class. However, one student is not fluent in multiplication. This student quickly loses

Misbehavior should not anger us but rather please us.

interest, views the task as hopeless, and engages in escape, avoidance, or attention-seeking behaviors. The teacher's typical response to the disruptions during independent seatwork activities is to punish the student.

It's important to ask ourselves if the goal is to have our students sit quietly holding a pencil, with their eyes on their papers, pretending to do work they cannot complete independently. Furthermore, is the use of punishment ethically appropriate when students lack the skills to perform the task?

Providing Direct Skill Training

Providing students with direct skill training is a fairly straightforward process that most teachers undertake every day. We break down the skill into its component parts, often referred to as subtasks. Then we instruct students on how to perform each subtask by modeling (sometimes while simultaneously giving instructions) the skill. Students rehearse the skill in isolation and may participate in role plays. Then we provide students with reinforcement. We often use corrective feedback—either verbal or physical prompts—when students fail to use the skill. Our goal in providing direct skill training is to move students from accuracy, through fluency, to automaticity.

In terms of managing resistance, we assume students will be compliant if they know how to perform the requested task or behavior. However, we know that this is not always the case. Many students know how to perform a task but choose to

be resistant. In these instances, it is helpful to have students engage in specific forms of practice.

Providing Specific Forms of Practice

Three interrelated practice techniques can help you manage resistance: overcorrection, negative practice, and inconvenience. All three of these techniques focus on changing the context surrounding undesirable behaviors. One of the two reoccurring themes of this book (the other one is that all behavior is purposeful) is that once we change the context surrounding a behavior, the meaning and purpose of that behavior changes and the student's desire to perform that behavior changes.

Overcorrection

The end result of overcorrection is the reduction or elimination of inappropriate behaviors. Typically considered a form of punishment, **overcorrection** is the repetition and exaggeration of an appropriate behavior. By spending time and effort engaging in the appropriate behavior students experience the inconvenience suffered by those who must otherwise correct the inappropriate behaviors.

There are two types of overcorrection: restitutional and positive practice. In **restitutional** overcorrection students are required to correct the effects of their inappropriate behaviors by restoring the environment to a state superior to that which existed before the misbehavior occurred. For example, a student who threw a piece of paper on the floor and refused to pick it up would be required to pick up all the paper on the floor.

Positive practice overcorrection involves having a student repeatedly practice an appropriate behavior that is related to the misbehavior. In this case, the student who threw the paper on the floor and refused to pick it up would be required to place the paper in a trash can repeatedly.

As behavior reduction techniques, both restitutional and positive practice overcorrection have enjoyed fairly good success rates. However, when it comes to managing resistance, we may be more skeptical—and for good reason. The obvious question is: If we cannot get a student to pick up a piece of paper after throwing it on the floor, how can we get her to either pick up all the paper in the room or repeatedly throw the paper in a trash can? The answer has little to do with the actual intervention. Rather, it focuses on the way we present the "practice" to the student. The key is to avoid a power struggle. In a matter-of-fact way, we explain to the student that we notice she has some difficulty putting paper in the trash can. Therefore, we say, she will devote 30 minutes to the practice of putting the paper in the trash can. We further state that different people require different amounts of practice time to learn skills in different areas. We are confident that she will be able to master the skill, but are uncertain if 30 minutes will be adequate time to practice and really learn to do it well. We suggest that we are always willing to let the student practice again if necessary.

In reality, the actual implementation of overcorrection—either restitutional or positive practice—is the *least important aspect of this technique*. Rather, overcorrection is a vehicle for helping us change our attitude and behavior toward a student who is noncompliant. We are enthusiastic and pleased that the student has the opportunity to practice. We convey that we are confident in her ability to catch on and we say that she can take her time to learn. This attitude ends the power struggle.

When we show frustration or anger students know that they have obtained power and control. Power and control are mighty reinforcers. In fact, the reinforcing value of a student obtaining power and control by being oppositional often prevails over the negative consequences. How many of us have heard ourselves say, "Are you trying to irritate me on purpose?" or "Do you like it when I get angry?" The answer to the first question is "yes" because there is reinforcing value in being able to get a rise out of another person. The answer to the second question is "no." Although the positive consequences of getting a reaction often outweigh the negative consequences, students still don't like the negative consequences. We need to respond to oppositional behavior in ways that do not give students power and control. If we really do not care that a student is spending 30 minutes picking up paper and, in fact, are pleased that she has the opportunity to practice and master the skill, the student will most likely not involve herself in a power struggle. After all, if she refuses, we will not be

If what you are doing is not working, try something else.

because of practicing. However, practicing picking up paper or making a bed for 30 minutes has never caused illness, death, or permanent disability. Besides, students have a choice in the matter—they can follow the direction and be done with it or they can practice.

The common concern we have about overcorrection or other novel techniques for managing resistance is what to do if they do not work. The answer is deceptively simple: try something else! Managing resistance is just as much attitude as it is technique. In fact, the two are interconnected. In the case of overcorrection, if the student refuses to practice, we can convey genuine sadness that she would bypass this option and then try something else. Many students would expect us to engage them in a power struggle over refus-

angry. If we really appear not to care, many students are likely to pick up the paper and be done with it.

The "I really don't care" attitude is difficult for many of us to assume. But it was not difficult for Erickson who used this technique often with his children. His daughter Kristina commented that she never felt that he minded if she spent a hundred hours practicing things—he was always pleased and hoped that she was enjoying herself (Zeig, 1985).

Erickson also never felt sorry for his children if they missed activities because of practicing. In fact, he would tell them what a great time they were missing. It is difficult for us to not sometimes feel sorry for students if they miss activities

ing to practice. By not feeding a power struggle, we increase the likelihood that the student will perform the practice. The refusal does not result in the student receiving power and control through our irritation.

Negative Practice

Both restitutional and positive practice overcorrection require students to practice the appropriate behavior. An alternative approach is negative practice. In **negative practice** a student is required to repeat the inappropriate behavior. For example, Azrin, Nunn, and Frantz (1980) treated the nervous tics of 22 institutionalized patients by requiring them to perform the tic in front of a mirror for 30-second periods during a one-hour session while simultaneously saying to themselves, "This is what I am not supposed to do." A caution is necessary before proceeding with this discussion: Negative practice should not be used for behaviors that are dangerous to self or others. A student who carves on her arm with a knife or hits peers should obviously not be instructed to repeatedly engage in these behaviors. Some professionals also object to the use of negative practice on the grounds that students should be taught appropriate behaviors and that negative practice only serves to focus undue attention on the misbehavior.

These criticisms are valid. However, negative practice serves an important function. It can change the context surrounding the inappropriate behavior, which, in turn, changes the meaning, purpose, and desire to perform it. In addition, it is fairly easy to get students to participate in negative practice because they are being instructed to engage in a behavior they want to perform. Here is an example of a teacher using negative practice (Maag, 1997):

An eighth grade student refused to complete a math worksheet assigned by the substitute teacher. Instead, the student wrote the name of his school followed by the word "sucks" all over his paper. Instead of encouraging the student to complete the assignment or giving a verbal reprimand, the teacher proceeded to set up the use of negative practice. She told the student that she was sorry he attended such a "sucky" school and that she was fortunate that, being a substitute, she did not have to spend much time in it. But more important, the substitute teacher pointed out that the student wasn't writing that his school sucked very creatively. The teacher also

commented that he had very distinctive handwriting, but that she was sure he could put it to more creative use. She suggested that the student try to write the two words in a variety of styles and colors. The student started in earnest, since he was being instructed to do what he was already doing. Shortly, he lost interest in the task and began to do the math assignment.

Erickson also used negative practice with one of his daughters:

My daughter came home from grade school and said, "Daddy, all the girls in school bite their nails and I want to be in style too."

I said, "Well, you certainly ought to be in style. I think style is very important for girls. You are way behind the girls. They have had a lot of practice. So I think the best way for you to catch up with the girls is to make sure you bite your nails enough each day. Now I think if you bite your nails for fifteen minutes three times a day, every day (I'll furnish a clock) at exactly such-and-such an hour, you can catch up."

She began enthusiastically at first. Then she began beginning late and quitting early and one day she said, "Daddy, I'm going to start a new style at school—long nails"
(Rosen, 1982, p. 145).

Erickson joined in his daughter's frame of reference and agreed that being in style was important. By agreeing with his daughter, Erickson created rapport: If his daughter wanted to be resistant, she would have to disagree with him that being in style was important, which would run counter to her frame of reference. Even if she disagreed with him by saying that being in style was not important, she would have been compliant because the goal was for her to not bite her nails. This "joining the child" is a prerequisite for getting compliance with the request to practice and again illustrates the nexus between technique and attitude. If Erickson had said, "Young lady, biting nails is a bad habit and you will be punished by having to spend fifteen minutes every day biting your nails to show you just how bad it is," his daughter most likely would have become resistant.

There is another important consideration when using negative practice: The behavior to be practiced should be one that a student cannot legitimately object to performing. In the previous two examples, the student and Erickson's daughter could not legitimately object to writing "sucks" or biting nails, respectively, because these were behaviors that they wanted to perform. Both were simply instructed, in an encouraging way, to do more of them.

Negative practice is an elegant intervention. The word elegance is used here to describe a technique that is simple and based on a student's existing frame of reference. Negative practice requires very little advanced preparation. The most difficult part of negative practice, as is also the case with overcorrection, is conveying to students that we are not angered but pleased that they have an opportunity to practice. This attitude goes against the typical mindset. We are accustomed to showing our displeasure towards inappropriate behaviors. Adopting a positive mindset, and having a behavior to which students cannot legitimately object, will add greatly to our ability to manage resistance with minimal effort. Otherwise, negative practice becomes punitive and meaningless.

Inconvenience

A final approach to practice is **inconvenience**. This approach can be used in conjunction with either overcorrection or negative practice. The idea is to change in some way the context surrounding the student's behavior. When the context is changed, so too is the meaning, purpose, and desire for the student to perform a behavior.

Many parents use this technique to get siblings to stop fighting. For instance, parents tell their children they can argue in the garage. Arguing is permitted, but it becomes troublesome to do so. Therapists often have couples use this same technique by instructing them to argue in a closet or car—anywhere that would be bothersome.

Erickson used this technique with his patients and his children. He was particularly creative in his use of inconvenience with his daughter Kristina (Zeig, 1985). Kristina recounted how she and her sister were in bed sleeping and Erickson came in the room and flipped on the lights in the middle of the night. He told Kristina how he had just noticed that the wheelbarrow and rake she had been using that day were in the middle of the backyard instead of in the garage where they belonged. Erickson told Kristina she would have to put them away. Still half asleep, she dragged herself out of bed, trudged into the backyard, put away the tools, and went back to bed while all along her sister was lamenting how her forgetfulness resulted in a disrupted night's sleep. After that, Kristina seldom forgot because she did not want to get up in the middle of the night again.

The important aspect of Erickson's use of inconvenience was that Kristina was never angry at him. For one thing, she knew she was supposed to put tools away after using them. For another, Erickson did not present the task as punishment.

He was apologetic about not noticing earlier that the tools were left outside. It is this attitude that helps us avoid a power struggle—there is nothing for a student to resist when we present the task as his or her own fault and apologize sincerely.

Let's look at a similar example in the classroom. A student has forgotten to put away the glue and scissors after completing an art project. The art teacher can wait until the student is at recess—a high preference activity—and approach him and apologetically (not angrily) explain that he just remembered the glue and scissors were left out. As they are walking inside, the teacher can reiterate his forgetfulness at not reminding the student at the end of the art activity. After that, most students will remember to put materials away to avoid the inconvenience of doing so during a fun activity.

Building Momentum

In some situations, students' old habits compete with their performance of newly acquired skills. Basically, certain contexts become cues or prompts for a student to engage in the old, habitual behaviors. For example, a student who has been taught how to ignore peers in order to get an assignment completed may have difficulty putting this new skill into practice when sitting next to a friend. In these cases, we can encourage students to be compliant by using three techniques that build momentum: embedding instructions, behavioral momentum, and the "Sure I Will" program.

Embedding Instructions

Instructions, as mentioned previously, are an important component of teaching students skills. A novel and effective variation of using instructions involves embedding. Embedding was used by Erickson to induce hypnotic trance (Bandler and Grinder, 1975) and has many nonhypnotic applications for managing resistance.

The essence of **embedding** is to instruct students to do what they are already doing while interspersing the request for the desired behavior. Here is an example of a teacher embedding an instruction: "Mary, shuffle your papers while you open your math book to page 18 and talk to Susie." In this situation, Mary is engaging in two undesirable behaviors: shuffling her papers and talking to Susie. This instruction embeds a new task between the two Mary is already performing. The teacher is trying to get Mary to comply with opening her math book to page 18. If the instruction was separated, Mary could easily refuse. But a refusal when the tasks are combined into a single instruction means what? That Mary will not shuffle her papers? That she will not open her book? That she will not talk to Susie? If Mary continues to be resistant by refusing to shuffle her papers and talk to Susie, then she is being compliant. If Mary stops what she is doing to smugly tell her teacher that she figured out her ploy, then she is also being compliant because she had to stop shuffling her papers and talking to Susie to do so. In essence, the teacher's instruction places Mary in

Trying and failing is not failing, it is assessment.
Never trying is failing.

a double bind in which she is forced to be compliant regardless of what she does.

There is another important factor in the effectiveness of this intervention: The student needs to expend great effort to identify the one task she is refusing to do. A refusal of the entire instruction cannot be offered comfortably. To the single tasks, she can easily say "no" to each. But to the combined task, she cannot say "no." If she is shuffling her papers, she must immediately open her book and talk to Susie. Hence, Mary may prefer to perform the combined task unwillingly rather than to put forth the effort to analyze the instruction minutely. This reasoning is specious, but it is the "emotional reasoning" that is common in daily life, and daily living is not an exercise in logic.

There are three common concerns teachers often voice over the use of embedding instructions. The first concern was addressed previously in the discussion of overcorrection—what if it does not work? Keep in mind that using a technique that does not work does not make you a "bad" teacher. It simply means the technique did not produce the desired outcome. At worst, the failure of a technique means we should try something else. At best, it gives us assessment information. The key consideration is to not take students' misbehavior personally. To do so gives students power and control—the power to get a reaction out of us. As discussed previously, power and control are extremely robust reinforcers, even when they elicit a negative reaction from us.

The second concern teachers voice about embedding involves showing Mary's classmates that we are condoning her noncompliant behavior by telling her to do what she is already doing: "If I tell Mary to shuffle her papers and talk to Susie, then everyone will want to shuffle their papers and talk to peers." This fear of contagion is

understandable but nonetheless spurious. Mary's classmates have seen her shuffle her papers and talk to Susie for many months—perhaps for most of the school year. The teacher's traditional approaches to engender compliance have failed. Observing Mary's behaviors did not prompt the other students to behave in the same fashion.

There are numerous examples of the "contagion concern." Recall the example in chapter 4 of the student with ADHD. His third-grade teacher gave him three chairs in order for him to discharge motor energy. His fourth-grade teacher refused to give him three chairs, stating that "if I give him three chairs, then everyone will want three chairs." Why would the other students want three chairs if they did not previously want to get out of their seat as often as the boy? Contagion only seems to be an issue when we are resistant to trying something different to solve the problems of resistance.

The third concern teachers often voice (and the one often used as the rationale for the second concern) is that by telling Mary to shuffle her papers and talk to Susie, we are condoning the inappropriate behaviors. In fact, we are not condoning inappropriate behavior. Mary is already performing the inappropriate behaviors and our traditional efforts have failed. This is an implicit form of condoning. If we tell Mary to stop talking and she refuses, what recourse do we have? Short of removing her from the room, we really can't make her stop talking. When a student refuses to stop a behavior after being instructed to, that's when we are condoning. We are conveying the message that our directions are meaningless.

By telling a student to do what she is already doing, the behavior comes under our control. When we can get one behavior under our control, it becomes easier to get subsequent behaviors under control because compliance momentum builds.

Behavioral Momentum

Behavioral momentum shares some similarities with embedding instructions. **Behavioral momentum** works by instructing a student to engage in two or three behaviors that we know he or she wants to perform, i.e., by making high probability requests. Once the student is performing the desired behavior, we make the low probability request. A low probability request is a request for a behavior that a student does not want to perform—typically the behaviors associated with following our instructions. For example, you may follow a request to have a student tack pictures on a bulletin board (high probability behavior) with the instruction to throw away trash (low probability behavior). The idea behind this approach is to build momentum toward compliance by first getting the student to perform a series of desired behaviors. Rhode, Jenson, and Reavis (1995) provided the following teacher guidelines for implementing behavioral momentum:

1. *Select a series of behaviors that a student already likes to do. That is, behaviors that the student is at least 70 percent likely to do when requested.*

2. *Ask the student to do several of the likely behaviors before asking the student to do the behavior he/she does not want to do (the unlikely behaviors). For example:*
   a. *"Tom, will you help me hand out the papers?"*
   b. *"Thanks Tom, now please help me straighten the chairs."*
   c. *"Now Tom, please sit down and do your math assignment."*

3. *Requesting two or three likely behaviors before requesting the unlikely behavior greatly enhances the momentum effect. However, asking even one likely behavior before the unlikely behavior can help, such as: "Tom, please help me erase the board" (likely behavior). "Now, Tom, please write your spelling word on the board" (unlikely behavior).*

4. *Behavior momentum can be engineered into your classroom schedule. Instead of starting with unlikely activities, such as a review of the previous day's problems, a difficult academic assignment, or calendar review, start with likely behavior games such as Simon Says, Seven-Up, a team guess of a teacher's selected mystery animal, reading a high interest story, charades, etc. Follow this activity with less likely activities (e.g., academic problem review) (p. 79).*

Behavioral momentum and embedding instructions are similar because they both link preferred behaviors with disliked behaviors. They are different in that, with embedding instructions, a student is first directed to do what he is already doing, whereas, with behavioral momentum, we request a behavior that is not being performed but that has a high probability of compliance. It is fairly easy to identify high probability behaviors—they are behaviors that students constantly request to perform. An example of a high probability behavior is when a student continually asks to empty shavings from the pencil sharpener.

Embedding instructions has a somewhat greater likelihood of obtaining a desired response because a student cannot refuse to do what she is already doing. (The student can only stop. In that case, the student is being compliant.) With behavioral

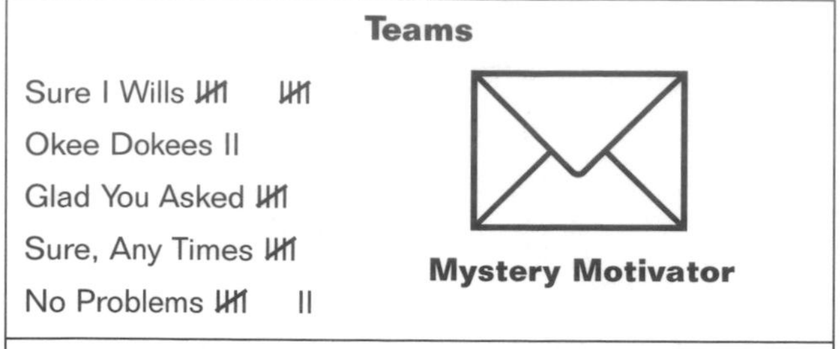

Teams

Sure I Wills 卌 卌
Okee Dokees ||
Glad You Asked 卌
Sure, Any Times 卌
No Problems 卌 ||

Mystery Motivator

Figure 2-3
Recording marks for teams on the blackboard in the "Sure I Will" program. *Note.* From *The Tough Kid Book* (p. 81), by Rhode, G.; Jenson, W.; and Reavis, K. (1992), Longmont, CO: Sopris West. Reprinted with permission.

momentum, we run the small risk that a student will not want to perform, for whatever reason, a high probability behavior upon request. The most likely reason behavioral momentum doesn't work in some cases is that we made too big a leap from the high probability request to the low probability request. The solution is fairly straightforward: task analyze the sequence of requests from high to low probability and provide the student with a "medium" probability request. For example, a teacher may ask a student to collect an assignment from a high status peer (medium probability request) after asking him to empty shavings from the sharpener (high probability request), but before asking him to throw away trash (low probability request).

The "Sure I Will" Program

The **"Sure I Will" program** involves teaching students a compliance-based behavior as a way to break a behavioral chain that would otherwise result in disobedience. This approach provides students with cues to perform desired behaviors. It builds momentum for following directions. In this approach, a student is taught to say "sure I will" after receiving a request. Compliance is then reinforced. Saying "Sure I will" interrupts the behavioral sequence that would otherwise maintain noncompliant behavior. Students can initially

be reinforced for saying "sure I will" at random times during the day, before specific requests are introduced. Through repetition and the occasional use of reinforcement, the words "sure I will" become habitual and are more likely to be spoken in response to a request in the future. Rhode et al. (1995) provided guidelines for implementing this intervention (see sidebar, p. 37).

Figure 2-3 illustrates how the "Sure I Will" program can be implemented as a group-oriented contingency (Step 4, a-g). The Mystery Motivator (Rhode et al., 1995) mentioned in Step 4 and shown in *Figure 2-3* is an envelope that contains slips of paper with highly preferred activities and privileges that students earn for answering with "Sure I will." The "Grab-Bag" is similar to the Mystery Motivator except that the listed reinforcers are placed in a bag instead of an envelope.

In addition, Rhode et al. (1995) described how this program can be combined with a response cost (i.e., fining students). In this case you would simply erase a point from the team whose member engaged in an inappropriate behavior or who refused to respond with "Sure I will." When using a response cost, the team should not lose more points than they earn, otherwise their motivation to participate decreases.

"Sure I Will"

1. The "Sure I Will" program is used with precision requests. The student must respond to a teacher's "Please" request with "Sure I Will" and start the behavior before the teacher issues the second request with the word need ("Now I need you to..."). If the student waits, he/she is not rewarded.

2. The student's "Sure I Will" response should always be socially rewarded by the teacher.

3. The student may also be rewarded randomly with a tangible reward such as academic points or a small toy.

4. The "Sure I Will" program can best be used with teams and a group contingency by following these steps:

   a. Each classroom team has a special response (e.g., "Sure I will," "Okey dokey," "Glad you asked," "Sure, any time," "No problem," etc.).

   b. The teacher selects a secret number each day that is unknown to the students (e.g., one day it might be 20, then 154, then 19) and writes it down on a piece of paper.

   c. The team's names are posted on the blackboard.

   d. The teacher makes a chalk mark by each team's name when a team member responds with his/her team's pre-selected verbal response and begins the behavior. For example, "Jeffrey, please sit down in your seat." "Sure I will, Mrs. Johnson," and he sits down.

   e. When the program first starts, the teacher should be liberal in recording marks for teams. However, after several days the teacher should only accept genuine efforts or sincere responses.

   f. At the end of each day, the teacher announces the secret number. If the number of a team's marks is the same or bigger than the secret number, the team gets to participate in the class reward (e.g., Mystery Motivator or Grab-Bag).

   g. If a team's number of marks is less than the secret number, they continue to do what is normally scheduled at that time of the day (p. 83).

Note. Adapted from *The Tough Kid Book* (p. 83) by Rhode, G.; Jenson W.R.; and Reavis, H.K., 1995, Longmont, CO: Sopris West. Reprinted with permission.

Chapter 6

Helping Students Who Have Pessimistic Expectations or Anxious Thoughts

(a Type 2 Prerequisite)

In order to address students' pessimistic expectations or anxious thoughts, we must first understand how these beliefs impact the performance of behaviors. Beliefs refer to self-statements or images that students hold about a given situation. They involve cognition. In the cognitive model of behavior presented in *Figure 2-4* **antecedents** refers to the events that precede and activate a belief. **Beliefs** are the ways students interpret, or give meaning to, an event or situation. **Consequences** are the outcome (the behavior or emotion).

The belief a student attaches to the antecedent will partially shape the consequences. [This model is the foundation of Ellis' Rational-Emotive Therapy (RET), described in greater detail in Part IV.]

In the cognitive model in *Figure 2-4*, beliefs play a significant role. Students' beliefs can be either rational or irrational. **Rational beliefs** are those that help students achieve their basic goals and purposes, and are logical and consistent with reality. **Irrational beliefs** are those that prevent students from achieving their basic goals and purposes, and are illogical and inconsistent with reality.

Although we do not know exactly how irrational beliefs are formed, there is consensus that they are based on a biological predisposition and, most importantly, past childhood experiences. Through past experiences, we develop **schema**—packets of information—that help us interpret, or make sense of, new experiences. We try to match new situations to established schemas by utilizing the concept of consistency.

Every situation we encounter is composed of a variety of stimuli that correspond to the senses: visual, auditory, olfactory, kinesthetic, gustatory, and proprioceptive (balance). If we are hang

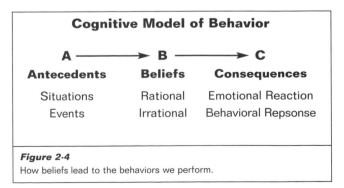

Cognitive Model of Behavior

A	→	B	→	C
Antecedents		**Beliefs**		**Consequences**
Situations		Rational		Emotional Reaction
Events		Irrational		Behavioral Repsonse

Figure 2-4
How beliefs lead to the behaviors we perform.

gliding for the first time, we would receive incoming visual stimuli (seeing the ground), auditory stimuli (hearing the wind over the wings), kinesthetic stimuli (feeling the glider), and proprioceptive stimuli (maintaining our balance).

The experience of hang gliding is also made up of a variety of other sense stimuli, but we selectively attend to stimuli related to relevant past experiences. If we attend to the variety of other visual stimuli around us (clouds, the position of the sun, the number of people on the ground watching us, etc.), we would most likely be distracted from the task at hand: remembering and practicing all the necessary skills for successfully flying and landing the hang glider.

We selectively attend to the stimuli that we deem important to our situation. If we attended to all the stimuli, we would feel overwhelmed, confused, and unable to make sense out of the situation—a disturbing state sometimes experienced by individuals with schizophrenia. Once we decide which stimuli are important, we must organize them in ways that give meaning to the experience.

Meaning is a function of context and past experiences. When we encounter new situations, we activate the schema we have used in the past. However, sometimes the normal matching of schema to a particular situation is upset: A schema that is inappropriate for a given situation is activated. Consequently, our interpretation of the situation is illogical and we overreact emotionally or engage in counterproductive behaviors. An important question, however, remains: How does mismatching between schema and situation occur in the first place? The best explanation is that mismatching is a learned process. For example, Wade may hold a belief that he did poorly on an addition facts quiz. When he gets his quiz back and sees he missed half the problems, he

says to himself, "Yep, I was right. I did poorly on this quiz." This is a correct, albeit negative, matching of schema (interpretation) and situation (score on the addition facts quiz). If Wade scores poorly on several more math quizzes, this schema becomes habitual and is accessed automatically. Wade learns to match this schema to this specific situation. He also learns to match it to similar situations.

If the schema proves to be correct in this one situation, there is a greater chance it will be automatically activated in other similar, yet slightly different, situations. This is because humans strive for consistency in their interpretations and interactions with others. Consistency breeds predictability, which leads to feelings of comfort and a sense of self-assurance. Because of the desire for consistency, Wade may activate the addition facts quiz schema in situations that are increasingly different from the original situation. Eventually, the schema is activated in situations that are so different from the original that they are dysfunctional. In this case, Wade would be activating the addition facts schema when faced with any math quiz. Then activating this schema when confronted with science quizzes. And so it goes...an irrational belief is born.

Following is a summary of how we form irrational beliefs:

1. We initially attach a correct but negative belief (or schema) to a particular situation.

2. If the schema proves to be correct in one situation, there is a greater likelihood that we will use it to interpret a wider range of situations.

3. The concept of consistency is responsible for our use of the same schema to interpret a wider range of situations.

4. As a schema becomes habitual, it is activated automatically, blocking the use of a more adaptive belief.

The main purpose of taking a cognitive approach to behavior is to help students replace an irrational belief with a rational one. This results in positive consequences—more satisfying emotional reactions and engagement in productive behaviors. Unfortunately, it can be extremely difficult to change students' beliefs. Once we hold a belief, it attains the status of fact. Even when we are presented with evidence that our belief is incorrect, we often tenaciously cling to it, probably because of the concept of consistency. Here is an example:

> Shano likes action movies and avoids movies heavy in dialogue because of the belief that they will be boring. Therefore, when his wife, Lorenna, suggests they see a romantic comedy, Shano believes it will be boring because it doesn't have much action. Yet, when they go to the movie, Shano is pleasantly surprised and enjoys it. Sometime later Lorenna wants to see another romantic comedy. Even though Shano had a positive experience seeing the first romantic comedy, his belief that movies without action are boring is activated. Again, when Shano sees the movie, he enjoys it. Yet when Loreena wants to see a third romantic comedy, Shano's belief remains the same as it was in the previous two situations.

It is extremely difficult to move students from their beliefs because their beliefs attain the status of facts. Therefore, getting students to consider alternative explanations requires creating rapport. You can establish rapport with your students by initially acknowledging their pessimism or negative beliefs. When you meet your students in their frames of reference, you can use their frames of reference to obtain a change in behavior.

Acknowledging Pessimism

The technique of acknowledging pessimism is deceptively simple: When a student says something negative or pessimistic about his or her performance, we agree! When we acknowledge a student's pessimism as real, the message conveyed is that his or her model of reality is understood. Acknowledgment makes it easier to get your students to realistically examine the validity of their pessimistic beliefs.

Never counter a student's pessimism with optimism, regardless of the good intentions behind comforting statements. Here is an example:

> *John may believe he will flunk a math test, even though the teacher knows John possesses the skills to pass. When a child has such a pessimistic belief, adults often counter with a statement such as, "Oh, that's ridiculous, you'll have no problem passing the test." Although this comment is meant to comfort John, it runs counter to his pessimistic belief and, therefore, creates resistance. John may say to himself, "My teacher doesn't understand me and is no help at all." Instead, the teacher should tell John, "I can understand your point, and it's probably better to be uncertain or doubtful at this time." This implies that the teacher recognized John's discouragement and validates it as being real, which, in turn, reduced resistance (Maag, 1997; p. 117).*

Once we create rapport by acknowledging pessimism, it is more likely that a student will follow a direction. In this case, the direction would be for John to examine the validity of his belief. However, we must choose our words carefully in this endeavor:

> *The teacher asks John, "Have there been any math tests that you almost flunked?" Notice the subtle phrasing used in this question: "almost flunked" is another way to say "passed." Using the word pass might have created resistance because John's belief involves flunking (Maag, 1997; p. 117).*

The purpose of the question is to get the student to put his pessimistic belief into perspective by comparing it to past experiences of success. John is more likely to reflect logically and respond honestly to this question once rapport has been created. If the teacher had first countered with optimism, John would have thought the teacher did not understand his position, and the teacher's question would have been ignored or answered insincerely.

At its simplest level, the technique of acknowledging pessimism is designed to seed ideas. In the previous example, if John answers the question about "almost flunking" with information that he once received a D+, the teacher could then ask if there was a time when he almost flunked as badly as receiving a D+? John might answer that he remembers receiving a C-. At this point, the teacher should not jump up and say "Ah ha, see you've never really flunked!" This response would undo the rapport established and likely recreate resistance. Simply having John acknowledge poor, but passing, grades seeds the idea that he has not flunked, nor will he likely flunk—no elaboration is necessary. Seeding ideas does not always have

an immediate effect. However, it creates a continuity in the therapeutic process. A new idea or piece of information is always introduced within a framework that connects it with previously accepted information.

Haley (1993) described a classic example of how Erickson acknowledged pessimism as a way to move a child's beliefs in a desired direction. In this story, Erickson's son Robert fell down the back stairs, split his lip, and knocked his upper tooth back into the maxilla. He was bleeding and screaming with pain and fright. His parents rushed to him and saw that it was an emergency:

> *No effort was made to pick him up. Instead, as he paused for breath for fresh screaming, he was told quickly, simply, sympathetically, and emphatically, "That hurts awful, Robert. That hurts terrible."*

> *Right then, without any doubt, my son knew that I knew what I was talking about. He could agree with me and he knew I was agreeing with him completely. Therefore, he could listen respectfully to me, because I had demonstrated that I understood the situation fully.*

> *Rather than reassure the boy, Dr. Erickson proceeded in typical fashion:*

> *Then I told Robert, "And it will keep right on hurting." In this simple statement, I named his own fear, confirmed his own judgment of the situation, demonstrated my good intelligent grasp of the entire matter and my entire agreement with him, since right then he could foresee a lifetime of anguish and pain for himself.*

> *The next step for him and for me was to declare, as he took another breath, "And you really wish it would stop hurting." Again, we*

were in full agreement and he was gratified and even encouraged in his wish. And it was his wish, deriving entirely from within him and constituting his own urgent need.

With the situation so defined, I could then offer a suggestion with some certainty of his acceptance. This suggestion was, "Maybe it will stop hurting in a little while, in just a minute or two."

This was a suggestion in full accord with his own needs and wishes and, because it was qualified by "maybe it will," it was not in contradiction to his own understanding of the situation. Thus, Robert could accept the idea and initiate his response to it.

Dr. Erickson then shifted to another important matter. As he puts it:

Robert knew that he hurt, that he was a damaged person; he could see his blood upon the pavement, taste it in his mouth and see it on his hands. And yet, like all other human beings, he too could desire narcissistic distinction in his misfortune, along with the desire for even more narcissistic comfort. Nobody wants a picayune headache; since a headache must be endured, let it be so colossal that only the sufferer could endure it. Human pride is so curiously good and comforting! Therefore, Robert's attention was doubly directed to two vital issues of comprehensible importance to him by the simple statements, "That's an awful lot of blood on the pavement. Is it good, red, strong blood? Look carefully, Mother, and see. I think it is, but I want you to be sure."

Examination proved it to be good, strong blood, but it was necessary to verify this by examination of it against the white background of the bathroom sink. In this way the boy, who had ceased crying in pain and fright, was cleaned up. When he went to the doctor for stitches the question was whether he would get as many as his sister had once been given. The suturing was done without anesthetic on a boy who was an interested participant in the procedure (pp. 6-7).

Note. From *Jay Haley on Milton H. Erickson* (pp. 6–7), by J. Haley, 1993, New York: Brunner/Mazel. Reprinted with permission.

We may think some of Erickson's comments to his son, such as "that hurts awful," and "it will keep right on hurting," to be cold, uncaring, and insensitive. After all, a common parental response would be to cradle the child and tell him everything will be alright. No matter how well-meaning this approach may be, it nevertheless creates resistance because it is not congruent with the child's frame of reference. Therefore, it will be more difficult to move the child in the desired direction. In Erickson's case, he wanted Robert to stop crying, follow him into the bathroom so that he could further examine his mouth, and then go to the hospital. Erickson's question of whether or not Robert would get as many stitches as his sister was a wonderful way to make positive use of sibling rivalry. As an adult, Robert reflected back upon the accident and his father's approach:

"When my father agreed with me, I realized that he clearly understood the pain I was experiencing, so I was ready to listen. My father had established credibility with me" (Erickson-Elliott et al., 1985, p. 628).

Don't Tell Me What To Do

It is important when working with others—students or adults—to not tell them what to do. We all have unique experiences that have been organized into equally unique sets of judgements about the nature of the world and the rules to live by. Telling someone what to do creates resistance because these statements are often contrary to his or her frame of reference. Try using questions instead. When we question others, we force them to deal with their reality, rather than imposing our reality on them.

Erickson's ability to accept patients' frames of reference and to seed ideas was truly amazing. Haley (1973) provided the following example:

> When Erickson was on the staff of Worcester State Hospital, there was a young patient who called himself Jesus. He paraded about as the Messiah, wore a sheet draped around him, and attempted to impose Christianity on people. Erickson approached him on the hospital grounds and said, "I understand you have had experience as a carpenter?" The patient could only reply that he had. Erickson involved the young man in a special project of building a bookcase and shifted him to productive labor (p. 28).

Erickson accepted the patient's belief that he was Jesus. The patient had no choice but to say he had experience as a carpenter if he wanted to maintain his delusion. By using the delusion, Erickson was able to lead the patient to meaningful and functional work—the initial step in recovery. The delusion of being Jesus served a useful function. Erickson simply used the delusion to get the patient engaged in appropriate work, thereby negating the patient's need for the delusion.

Setting Up a Small Change in Behavior

Students who hold negative beliefs—or have any propensity to be resistant—are more likely to comply with a request to make a small, rather than large, change in their behavior. Managing resistance does not have to be a taxing endeavor. Sometimes we set our standards higher for students with challenging behaviors than we do for those without behavior problems. It is almost as if we achieve a sense of control or security, albeit false, from expecting students with challenging behaviors to behave better than children without behavior problems. Here is an example:

> A consultant was assisting a teacher who was scheduled to have a student with a behavior disorder mainstreamed into his classroom for 2 1/2 hours every morning. The teacher stated that his main concern was that this student would get out of her seat too many times without permission and disrupt other students. When the consultant asked the teacher how many times he could tolerate the student getting out of her seat during the course of a morning, the teacher replied "once."

Behavior change is like a kaleidoscope: Once the tube is turned even a fraction of an inch, the entire pattern changes.

The consultant spent the week observing the teacher and the class. Whenever any student got out of his or her seat without permission, the consultant glanced at the teacher. If the teacher ignored the student (that is, tolerated the student being out of his or her seat), the consultant made a tally mark on an observation sheet. At the end of the week the consultant added the tally marks and divided this number by the number of students in class; thereby calculating the average number of times each student got out of his or her seat without permission but was tolerated. The average number was six—even though the teacher stated he could only tolerate one out-of-seat for the student with the behavior disorder. Who, then, had the problem? It was the teacher's inappropriately high standard that interfered with his ability to manage resistance effectively.

This example not only demonstrates the biasing effect of labels, but also demonstrates how labels interfere with our ability to set realistic standards and to "think small." The solution is to set small goals for students and then reinforce their successive progress toward the goals. Behavior is not performed in one instance. It needs to be shaped through a step-by-step process that develops a new, positive behavior by reinforcing closer approximations of it. The goal of shaping is to guarantee students comply and experience success. Keep in mind that disruptive or noncompliant behav-

1	2	3	4
Stimulus	**Response**	**Stimulus**	**Response**
math quiz	anxiety	crying	run out of room

Figure 2-5
Interjecting a request that the student be anxious between Step 1 and Step 2 would create sequence confusion, thereby changing the outcome.

iors have become habitual in some student's lives and are difficult to change immediately. If a student is chronically late to class by ten minutes or more, she should be praised when she makes it through the door in five minutes. Once she begins to make improvements in the desired direction, future behavior changes become much easier. Requiring small changes in behavior set in motion larger changes.

The goal of "thinking small" is to make it impossible for a student to be resistant. Because the initial request is so small it is meaningless to resist. If the task is small and we are still getting resistance, then the student is probably reacting to our behavior.

Obtaining a small change in behavior alters a student's behavior pattern enough to achieve persist-

ent and increasingly functional results. From a behavioral perspective, the performance of a behavior can be conceptualized in terms of a **stimulus-response chain**. A stimulus elicits a response which, in turn, becomes a cue to perform another behavior. For example, a traffic light that turns from yellow to red is a cue to take your foot off the accelerator. The behavior of removing your foot from the accelerator then becomes a cue to depress the brake.

Sequence confusion (initiating a small alteration in the sequence) interrupts the stimulus-response chain (Lankton, 1985). In *Figure 2-5*, a student feels anxious when he walks into a classroom to take a math quiz. Anxiety then becomes a cue for him to begin crying. Crying, in turn, becomes a cue for him to run out of the room. However, if the sequence of the stimulus-response chain is changed, the student can no longer perform the behavior as it was previously. Instructing the student to "feel anxious" 15 minutes prior to class scrambles the sequence of the stimulus-response chain (creating sequence confusion). In this example the intervention is paradoxical—if the student is able to comply and bring on feelings of anxiety, then he has proof that the anxiety is under his control. If he refuses to bring on the anxiety, he also has proof that the anxiety is under his control.

There are many ways we can create small changes in behavior utilizing sequence confusion (sometimes called paradoxical injunction or creating ordeals). Some of these approaches, like inconvenience, have been described previously. Others are discussed in subsequent chapters. The important point to keep in mind now is that students will almost always find making small changes more agreeable than making large changes. Gordon and Meyers-Anderson (1981)

said about Erickson: "By making his interventions at seemingly unrelated or trivial places and in innocuous ways, Erickson avoids an unproductive and unnecessary clash of wills" (p. 121). This same mentality can be used in the classroom. Here is an example of how a consultant helped a teacher set up a small change in behavior:

> A teacher was having difficulty getting a student, Guillermo, to complete his math assignments. The consultant was warned by the principal that the teacher was frustrated, had given up on the student, and refused to try anything that would take time away from the other students who wanted to learn. Every day after presenting a formal math lesson, the teacher would pass out worksheets with about 20 problems for students to complete during the last 15 minutes of class. Guillermo did not understand the work at the beginning of the year, was later sick and out of school for two weeks, and took another several weeks upon his return before he finally began grasping the material. However, by that time, he had accumulated about 30 incomplete math worksheets in a folder. Guillermo felt "behind the eight ball" and knew he could never catch up. Therefore, he obtained attention and power and control, and escaped from working on the assignments by misbehaving.

> The consultant asked the teacher what she wanted from Guillermo. She replied that she wanted him to stop running around the classroom, disrupting other students while they were completing their math worksheets. (It is amazing how often we are better able to tell others what we *do not* want from students!) When asked

what she wanted Guillermo to do instead, the teacher replied that she wanted him to sit quietly in his seat. (Often we go from wanting our students to stop misbehaving to wanting them to not behave at all!) When asked what she wanted Guillermo to do if he was sitting quietly, the teacher replied that she wanted him to complete his math assignment. She was then asked what she wanted if Guillermo could not complete the entire assignment. She said she wanted him to at least complete some of the assignment.

Through these questions, the consultant eventually ascertained what it was the teacher desired. She wanted Guillermo to complete some of the assignment.

The consultant then asked the teacher what type of math problems she wanted the student to complete. She responded that the worksheets focus on one-digit to two-digit multiplication. The consultant then gave the teacher a worksheet with one multiplication problem on it and told her to tell the student that when he finished his worksheet he could have free time for the remainder of the class period. The teacher quickly responded that that approach was unacceptable. However, the consultant pointed out that if the student completed the recommended worksheet his performance would increase 100 percent—not a bad first result!

So often we overlook the fact that getting any change in a student's behavior pattern has a future, positive, therapeutic value. We lament the oppositional nature of a student who tweaks an adjacent peer's ear after being told to stop poking the peer's arm. What we fail to appreciate is that we were able to get a change in the pattern of behavior! Granted, the change was from one negative behavior to another, but change nonetheless occurred. It may not be a positive, lasting change, but the student still responded to our intervention. That response teaches us something about the interaction between the intervention and the student.

All students communicate with us about how to deal with them effectively. The key is to be comprehensive in our repertoire and live the axiom "If what you are doing is not working—try something else." Trying and failing is not failing—it is assessment; never trying is failing. When we are able to assume this attitude and not take students' misbehavior personally, we access many options for managing resistance. These two points are further elaborated in Part IV.

Using a Force-Field Analysis

The force-field analysis technique was developed by social psychologist Kurt Lewin as a strategy for managing resistance to change. Lewin is credited with developing field theory, which states that human behavior is a function of the person and the environment or social situation in which he or she is interacting. Lewin conceptualized

---

The 3 Steps of Force-Field Analysis:

1. Help the student list all possible avoidance behaviors (resisting forces).
2. Help the student list all possible approach behaviors (driving forces).
3. Plan with the student ways to reduce the number and impact of the avoidance behaviors and increase the number and impact of the approach behaviors.

Figure 2-6
Use force-field analysis to achieve compliance with your students.

conflicts as falling into one of three categories: approach-approach, avoidance-avoidance, or approach-avoidance. In force-field analysis, the teacher assists the student in listing all possible avoidance behaviors (called "resisting forces") and all possible approach behaviors ("driving forces"). Next, the teacher and student plan ways to reduce the number and impact of the avoidance behaviors and increase the number and impact of the approach behaviors. In **approach-approach** the student is exposed to two similar forces that have positive features. In **avoidance-avoidance**, the student is exposed to similar forces that have negative features. In **approach-avoidance** the student is exposed to opposing forces that possess both positive and negative features. An example of approach-avoidance conflict is illustrated by this moral dilemma:

> *Sharon and Jill were best friends. Once day they went shopping together. Jill tried on a sweater and then, to Sharon's surprise, walked out of the store wearing the sweater under her coat. A moment later, the store's security officer stopped Sharon and demanded that she tell him the name of the girl who had walked out. He told the storeowner that he had seen the two girls together, and that he was sure that the one who left had been shoplifting. The storeowner told Sharon that she could really get in trouble if she didn't give her friend's name (Beyer, 1976, pp. 194-195).*

The moral dilemma presented both positive and negative features to Sharon. Should she avoid telling the storeowner to maintain her relationship with Jill (approach)? Or should Sharon tell the storeowner to avoid placing herself at risk for criminal prosecution (avoidance)? This situation creates considerable **cognitive dissonance** (a state in which a person holds two beliefs or cognitions that are inconsistent with each other). This type of cognitive dissonance formed the basis for Lewin's force-field analysis intervention and provided the rationale for including it in classroom behavior management.

In Step 1 of *Figure 2-6*, we could easily list all the avoidance behaviors in which a student engages. However, it is more effective to have the student perform this task, since it takes advantage of his or her resistant point of view. Having the student brainstorm all the possible reasons and ways to be noncompliant serves two purposes. First, by listing ways to avoid the task, the student is actually being cooperative. That is, the student is following our direction. Once the student is compliant in one area, it is easier to obtain compliance in other areas. Force-field analysis is paradoxical because in order for the student to resist, he or she must comply. The second purpose the brainstorm serves is to change the surrounding context of the resistant behavior. Changing the context changes the meaning of the behavior and also the purpose and desire for engaging in it.

In some instances, it is not necessary to perform Step 2 (listing approach behaviors) because during Step 1 the student realizes no power and control or attention payoff will be gained from continuing to be resistant. But when Step 2 is warranted, the student is more likely to comply because compliance was already attained by first listing avoidance behaviors. Basically, by first listing avoidance behaviors that are congruent with the student's resistant frame of reference, behavioral momentum is created for the student to comply with other directions.

We can reduce the number of occurrences of avoidance behaviors and their impact, while increasing the number of occurrences of approach

> *Don't be afraid of opposition.*
> *Remember, a kite rises against the wind, not with it.*

behaviors and their impact, by using the avoidance behaviors as reinforcers. The student can attain the reinforcers by first performing the approach behaviors. This approach makes use of the **Premack principle** (described in more detail in Part III), which states that access to a desired behavior or activity is contingent upon the performance of a less desirable behavior or activity (Premack, 1959). Following is an example of a force-field analysis:

Tricia is a student who is part of a cooperative learning group assigned the task of sharing information from a social studies chapter in order for the group to complete the activity. Instead of sharing information and helping the group, Tricia is doodling on a piece of paper, brushing her hair, and talking to other group members about her favorite music groups.

Her teacher responds in the typical, ineffective way: a cycle of escalating consequences. This approach provides Tricia with power and control over the teacher (i.e., Tricia knows she is pushing the teacher's buttons) and attention from peers she did not previously experience. Using a force-field analysis, the teacher says:

"Tricia, I see that you're avoiding the assignment by doodling, brushing your hair, and talking about unrelated subjects." (This response creates rapport since the teacher is mirroring what the student is doing instead of reprimanding her.)

"And I see that you've become pretty good at avoiding this assignment." (How can a student object to this comment without becoming compliant?) "But you know what? I think there are a lot of other creative ways for you to avoid completing this assignment. What are some of the things you've done in the past to avoid completing the assignment? I'm very interested in hearing all those ways."

Tricia's off-task behaviors did not anger the teacher. Rather, the teacher was pleased that Tricia's behavior provided an opportunity to list additional ways to avoid the assignment. By listing all the ways of avoiding the task (e.g., wandering around the room, sharpening her pencil, getting a drink, or using the restroom), Tricia is being compliant. Any power and control value Tricia may have obtained from being off-task was effectively short-circuited. There is also little or no attention payoff for Tricia because the other students observe that her behavior does not irritate the teacher. Tricia may then choose to comply with the task, or at least be more receptive to listing approach behaviors, because compliance momentum has already been established. After listing the compliance behaviors, the teacher could proceed to Step 3:

"Tricia, you just told me that you could help get this assignment finished by sharing information with the group, asking questions, writing answers, and talking only about the task. That gives me an idea. If you help your group by doing those behaviors for 15 minutes, then I'll give you 5 minutes to brush your hair, talk about anything you wish, wander around the room, get a drink, or use the restroom."

In this example, the teacher uses the avoidance behaviors to reinforce the approach behaviors— that is, she makes use of the Premack principle. Rapport is developed using Tricia's resistant frame of reference by first acknowledging that she is engaging in off-task behaviors and then encouraging her to list additional ways to be off-task. Again, once compliance is achieved in one area, it becomes easier to lead the student in the direction of the desired outcome.

Resistance does not have to be feared. It can be used to engender compliance. The more resistant a student, the easier it is to obtain compliance. This statement may sound unbelievable, but it is based on the notion that we should use resistance, not avoid it.

Resistant behavior gives us valuable information about how to react in a way that is congruent with the student's frame of reference, so that we can create rapport and obtain a desired outcome. Students will always communicate to us how to deal with them effectively. We need to remember to listen and not be paralyzed by our own paradigm.

PART III

Function Over Form

Behavior does not occur in a random or unorganized fashion. Students behave purposely, and their behavior attains meaning as a function of the **context** (the situation or circumstance that exists in a particular environment). The **environment** refers to the events and objects that are part of the surroundings. A classroom is comprised of **objects**—animate objects (such as students and adults) and inanimate objects (including tables, chairs, blackboards, and materials). Objects also include **social norms** and **cultural mores** (social manifestation of norms). Social norms and cultural mores have a profound influence on student behaviors and how we interpret them.

Chapter 7

The Impact of Environment on Behavior

Events are part of the environment—a fire drill, a final examination, and all the daily occurrences. Each event happens in relation to other events. This relation between events is called a contingency. A **contingency** is an event that depends on the fulfillment of a condition or prior occurrence. Contingencies can be identified and modified. Modifying contingencies can have a profound effect on behavior. To do this, we need to first look at the antecedents and consequences that contribute to the behavior.

Antecedents are the circumstances that exist in the environment *before* a behavior is exhibited. Antecedents exist for all behaviors and serve as cues or prompts for us to behave in particular ways. For example, a red traffic light is an antecedent that prompts us to depress the brake. Other examples of antecedents include the ringing of a phone as a cue for us to answer it, asking a question as a cue for a student to provide an answer, or smiling at someone as a cue for that individual to smile back or say "hello." It is important to understand that antecedents do not cause behaviors—they only serve as prompts. There is no inherent biological predisposition to depress a brake when we encounter a red traffic light—it is a learned behavior. The red light cannot prevent us from choosing instead to depress

the accelerator. But antecedents cue us to engage in specific behaviors that help us to either avoid punishment or obtain reinforcement. Most of us stop at a red light in order to avoid the potential consequences of receiving a ticket or getting into an accident. Although our behaviors are cued by antecedents, they are ultimately controlled by consequences.

Consequences change the environment shortly after a behavior is exhibited. Consequences affect the future performance of behavior by punishing or rewarding. There are two forms of consequences:

1. After a behavior is exhibited, a new stimulus is presented or added to the environment (e.g., student receives 10 minutes of free time for completing a math assignment).

The A-B-C Model

A	B	C
Antecedents	**Beliefs**	**Consequences**
People & Events	Appropriate	Reinforcement
	Inappropriate	Punishment

Figure 3-1.
The environment's impact on behavior

---

2. After a behavior, an already present stimulus is avoided, terminated, or removed from the environment (e.g., the teacher stops standing over a student when he or she finishes a math assignment).

Figure 3-1 illustrates the context in which behavior occurs. It is different from the cognitive model that appears in *Figure 2-4*. Although both models share an A-B-C format and similar antecedents, the model in *Figure 3-1* is concerned with the environment's impact on behavior, whereas the cognitive model in *Figure 2-4* is concerned with the impact of beliefs on our emotions and behavior. Both models are helpful, but serve very different roles in the process of managing resistance.

When observing a behavior using the A-B-C Model in *Figure 3-1*, we write down the sequence of events—the circumstances preceding a behavior, the behavior itself, and the circumstances following the behavior. *Table 3-1* shows how behaviors are analyzed using the A-B-C Model. In the first example, the teacher's question serves as a cue for Audre to provide the answer. Audre's behavior—giving the correct answer—prompts a new stimulus into the environment—teacher praise. Assuming Audre values teacher praise, the consequence will likely maintain or increase her behavior (answering questions). In the second example, Jimmy finds it aversive to be called a jerk by Billy. This antecedent serves as a cue for Jimmy to hit Billy. The consequence is that Billy stops calling Jimmy a jerk—an already present stimulus is terminated.

In Example 3 Miguel successfully avoids the stimulus (the spelling test) by getting a stomachache.

Learning took place in all of these examples. Example 2 also illustrates how aggressive behaviors quickly get students what they want, making it difficult for us to get them to stop. Note that although these examples are presented in a linear fashion, behavior is interactive and continuous. In the first example, the consequence of the teacher telling Audre she gave a great answer may be the antecedent for the subsequent behavior of Audre saying "thank you," which, in turn, prompts the consequence of the teacher saying "you're welcome." The teacher's response then begins another interaction sequence.

Later in Part III, functional assessment is discussed. Functional assessment will help you test

---

	Antecedent	Behavior	Consequence
Example	1 Teacher asks Audre a question.	Audre gives correct answer.	Teacher tells Audre she gave a great answer (stimulus presented).
	2 Billy calls Jimmy a jerk.	Jimmy hits Billy.	Billy stops calling Jimmy a jerk (stimulus terminated).
	3 Spelling test is given.	Miguel gets a stomachache.	Miguel is sent to nurse (stimulus avoided).

Table 3-1.
Using the A-B-C Model to analyze behavior.

each antecedent to see which one has the greatest impact on a target behavior.

The A-B-C Model explains the majority of learned behavior. Take for example a toddler who is learning to eat independently for the first time. The antecedent is the parent placing a plate of food on the tray of the highchair. This antecedent is followed by several behaviors: the toddler putting food in her mouth, smearing food on her clothes, and throwing food on the floor. The consequence for throwing food on the floor is that the parent picks up the food, feeds the toddler, and tells the toddler that food goes in the mouth. As a result, the toddler learns that she can get attention by throwing food on the floor and get the parent to feed her. An alternative consequence the parent could employ is to ignore the toddler when she throws food and give attention when she places food in her mouth. In this scenario, the toddler learns that parental attention comes when food is placed in the mouth and not when it is thrown on the floor. The point is that antecedents and consequences shape the behavior and whether or not that behavior will be performed in the future.

Rearranging the Environment to Promote Compliance

In terms of managing resistance, we often spend considerable time focusing on student behavior. Although there is valuable information that we can obtain regarding a student's ability to comply with a request, this focus is unduly narrow. In many instances, effective interventions do not focus solely on a student, but involve analyzing and rearranging the environment to promote compliance.

The techniques that follow in Chapter 8 and Chapter 9 focus on manipulating antecedents and consequences. **Antecedent manipulations** include:

1. Arranging cues to make compliance behaviors more visible

2. Changing the pattern or routine surrounding the performance of a behavior.

Consequent manipulations include:

1. Finding effective reinforcers

2. Reducing competing sources of reinforcement.

Chapter 8
___

Antecedent Manipulations

One of the most important antecedent manipulations that relies on arranging cues to make compliance more visible is self-monitoring. Self-monitoring, like other approaches that change the pattern of antecedents, builds on the contextual manipulation techniques described in Part II. By eliminating the antecedent that promoted the inappropriate behavior and replacing it with a new antecedent, you can prompt appropriate behavior.

Teaching Self-Monitoring

Some cues exert a powerful control over behavior. Others have no appreciable effect. For example, the ring of a phone almost always elicits our picking up of the receiver and saying "hello." On the other hand, receiving a piece of junk mail rarely elicits the behavior of opening and reading it. There are limitless variables in the environment that can cue students to engage in noncompliant behaviors. For example, receiving a math assignment may cue a student to make animal noises as a way to avoid the work or to obtain the attention of peers. Or a student who writes a note to himself as a reminder to do his homework has provided himself with a cue.

Some students are resistant when they are not able to read the cues their peers are responding to. For example, when a teacher picks up a spelling book, it is often a cue for students to take out a piece of paper for a test. It is rarely necessary for the teacher to give the instruction to take out a piece of paper. Or, a student may not pick up on a stern look from the teacher to stop talking. Any type of symbol that provides an extra or more salient cue will help prompt compliance. Notes or pictures can be used to depict activities in which students are supposed to engage. For example, a student may remember to continue

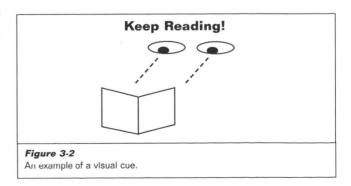

Keep Reading!

Figure 3-2
An example of a visual cue.

reading independently when she has the cue appearing in *Figure 3-2* taped to her desk.

One of the most efficient ways to provide students with salient cues while also promoting independence is to teach students to self-monitor. **Self-monitoring** means students observe and record their own behaviors. This technique often results in **reactivity**—the process whereby observing and recording one's own behavior changes that behavior in the desired direction.

Self-monitoring has been used with students with and without disabilities, ranging in age from four years old to adolescence, in a variety of settings, including special and general education classrooms, psychiatric hospitals, and residential facilities. In school settings, self-monitoring has been used successfully to improve academic achievement in reading, spelling, and mathematics and to decrease inappropriate social behaviors, such as aggression and inattention. Not only has self-monitoring proven to be effective, it can also be

easily incorporated into existing classroom structures and activities.

There are a variety of approaches for teaching students to self-monitor their behavior, academic performance, use of problem-solving strategies, or attention to task. The approach you take depends on the behaviors of concern, the student's maturity, and the situation. In the case of managing resistance, self-monitoring attention (SMA) can be used to cue students to observe and record a variety of compliance behaviors.

Self-monitoring attention (SMA) involves instructing students to observe their own behavior, determine whether or not they are being compliant, and record the results when cued through the use of randomly presented tones from a tape recorder or computer application. This procedure was developed by Hallahan, Lloyd, and Stoller (1982) and consists of four major parts:

1. Random tape-recorded or computer-generated tones to cue the student to self-monitor

2. A self-questioning strategy the student uses when self-monitoring

3. A recording form the student uses to mark answers to the self-monitoring questions

4. A self-monitoring graph the student uses to chart progress.

Materials needed for implementing SMA include a self-monitoring tape or computer application (see Related Resources section), a self-monitoring card, and a worksheet with a bar graph. Implement SMA while students are engaged in a productive activity, such as working independently, playing a group game, or doing chores.

Self-Monitoring Cues

It is important to provide an auditory cue for students to self-observe and self-record their behavior. A tape of random tones or a computer application can be purchased, or you can create a tape by following the guidelines on "Recording a Self-Monitoring Tape" in the Reproducibles section.

Self-Monitoring Cards

Reproducible self-monitoring cards like the ones in *Figure 3-3* and *Figure 3-4* are provided in the Reproducibles section. These cards have a place for students to write their names, the date, and the description of the target behavior (defining compliance). Students indicate whether or not they are being compliant in the squares. The reproducible for younger students includes pictures of happy and sad faces instead of the words "yes" and "no" in each column. Rather than writing the description of the target behavior, you might draw a picture, like the one in *Figure 3-2*, as a visual cue.

There are a limitless number of target behaviors that can be written on the self-monitoring cards: following directions, asking a question, answering a question, eyes on work, or saying "sure I will." Two important considerations when deciding on target behaviors are:

Self-Monitoring Card

Name <u>Billy Jones</u>   Date <u>March 15</u>

WAS I FOLLOWING DIRECTIONS

When you hear the beep, ask yourself if you are:
Following directions or working on a task.
If the answer is yes to any of these, place a check in the **"Yes"** column. If the answer is no, place a check in the **"No"** column.

	YES	NO		YES	NO
1.	x		13.		x
2.		x	14.		x
3.		x	15.	x	
4.	x		16.		x
5.		x	17.	x	
6.	x		18.	x	
7.	x		19.		x
8.	x		20.	x	
9.		x	21.	x	
10.	x		22.	x	
11.		x	23.		x
12.		x	24.	x	

Number of "X"s in **YES** column____

Figure 3-3
Once the self-monitoring card is completed, the student counts up the tally marks in the "Yes" column and graphs the number. In this way, the student can see his or her progress and set goals for the next self-monitoring session.

1. The behaviors are easy to define (so that all school personnel can observe them similarly)

2. No more than three behaviors are listed (so that a student will not be confused).

Two behaviors were selected for the self-monitoring card in *Figure 3-3:* following directions and working on the task. Both of these behaviors need to be specifically defined for the student. For example, you might define "following directions" as engaging in the requested behavior within 10 seconds after receiving the instruction. You might define "working on the task" as writing answers and keeping eyes on the materials.

Make a mark beside the day of the week every time you follow a direction without being told twice.		
		Total
Monday	III	3
Tuesday	ЖТ	5
Wednesday	ЖТ IIII	9
Thursday	ЖТ II	7
Friday	ЖТ ЖТ II	12
Grand Total		36

Name: <u>Roger Anderson</u>   Week: <u>April 8 - April 11</u>

Figure 3-4
Example of a self-monitoring card without auditory cues.

Self-monitoring cards can also be used without self-monitoring tapes. For example, the self-monitoring card in *Figure 3-4* (also included in the Reproducibles section) simply requires a student to make a tally mark every time he or she follows a direction. In this instance, the self-monitoring card itself serves as a cue for the student to self-monitor and make a mark. As in the previous examples, "following directions" needs to be specifically defined for the student prior to implementation.

The Self-Monitoring Graph

Having students graph the totals appearing on their self-monitoring cards increases reactivity. Graphs allow students to compare their performance from day to day (or session to session) which, in turn, helps them to evaluate their performance and praise themselves. A blank graph is provided in the Reproducibles section. At the end of the self-monitoring session, students tally their marks in the "yes" or

"happy face" columns for the days of the week and color in the number of boxes on the graph. This process is analogous to a thermometer. As compliance increases, more of the bar is shaded; and as compliance drops, less of the bar is shaded.

Figure 3-5 shows a completed graph of the self-monitoring card example in *Figure 3-4*. The vertical axis of the graph is labeled "Number of times I followed directions." Note that it is more desirable for the student to focus on the positive aspect of following directions rather than on the number of times he or she did

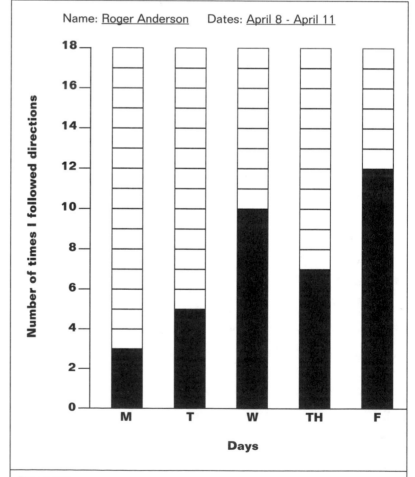

Figure 3-5
Bar Graph for Number of Times Following Directions.

> *Going to therapy is like having someone spit in your soup.*
> *You can continue to eat it, but you can't enjoy it.*

not follow directions. In this case the horizontal axis is marked for "Days," but it can be marked for "Sessions," depending on whether self-monitoring is scheduled more than once a day.

You can teach your students the steps of self-monitoring in about 15 or 20 minutes (depending on their ages and cognitive abilities) following the "Self-Monitoring Procedures" in the sidebar on page 62. Self-monitoring is most appropriate for noncompliant behaviors that have become habitual from repeated use. For example, Tim may repeatedly swear in class. Unfortunately swearing is a normal verbal behavior for Tim's peer group and family. Therefore, Tim is resistant to stopping this behavior because he is not aware that he is swearing. Having Tim self-monitor his swearing will increase his awareness of this behavior. In essence, self-monitoring can help take unconscious automatic behaviors and bring them into the conscious realm. It becomes easier to help Tim stop swearing once he is aware of engaging in this behavior.

Changing Patterns and Routines

Students develop patterns of behavior and routines specific to certain contexts or situations. In Part II several approaches (negative practice, inconvenience, setting up a small change in behavior) were introduced that conceptualized the performance of behavior in terms of a stimulus-response chain. These approaches focus on rearranging the stimulus-response chain so that the behavior can no longer be performed (prompted) as it was previously.

A stimulus can be anything that is introduced into the environment. In some instances, another person's **behavior** is a stimulus that elicits a response. For example, a person extending her hand in greeting is a cue to shake it.

In other instances, our own behavior can be a stimulus for us to perform a subsequent behavior. For example, depressing the clutch on the car is a cue to then shift gears.

Context can also prompt certain behaviors. The context of attending a baseball game elicits different behaviors than the context of attending a business meeting. Context is how behavior obtains its social meaning. Changing context (described in Part II as sequence confusion) has the effect of changing the meaning, purpose, and desire for engaging in a behavior (as depicted in *Figure 1-4*).

Recall in Chapter 2 the study described by Ayllon (1963): A psychiatric patient hoarded and stored large numbers of towels in her room. By giving her an increasing number of towels daily, Ayllon repeatedly exposed the patient to the antecedents of her inappropriate behavior. This approach is called **stimulus saturation**. Since receiving one towel served as a cue for the patient to hoard it, removing towels from her room would give the patient power, control, and attention. However, by giving the patient an increasing number of towels, the context surrounding the behavior changed. Hoarding no longer had the meaning it previously held. Consequently, the patient no longer obtained power, control, and attention from the staff for this behavior. The patient could,

Self-Monitoring Procedures

1. Provide your students with a rationale for self-monitoring (e.g., it will help them get work done quicker).

2. Obtain a commitment from your students to try self-monitoring.

3. Present the self-monitoring materials to your students (cards, tape player, and graphs).

4. Define the specific target behaviors and model instances of compliance and noncompliance.

5. Explain that the tape to be played has tones on it.

6. Tell your students to ask themselves if they were being compliant when the tone sounds. If the answer is yes, they make a mark in the "Yes" or "happy face" column. If the answer is no, they make a mark in the "No" or "sad face" column.

7. Show your students how to tally their self-monitoring cards and graph the number of "yes" marks at the end of each session.

8. Have your students paraphrase and explain to you how the procedure works.

9. Demonstrate the procedure, asking students to watch to make sure you self-monitor correctly.

10. While demonstrating the procedure, make some incorrect marks and see if the students catch them.

11. Have your students practice the procedure while you give feedback. Repeat this process until the students can perform self-monitoring independently.

of course, continue to hoard, but it no longer had the same meaning.

Saturating a student with the antecedents of a behavior is a way of surpassing his or her tolerance level for the behavior. Each student has a personal tolerance level of how much to perform a behavior, whether that behavior is appropriate or inappropriate. By giving a student who continuously doodles on worksheets an increasing number of worksheets every week, we saturate him or her with the antecedent stimulus. When the student burns out on the stimulus of receiving an increasing number of worksheets, he or she will change the behavior on his or her own. The student can continue to doodle, but won't like doing so because the amount of doodling exceeds his or her tolerance level.

Pattern Reversal

Reversing patterns, or looking at things in the reverse, was one of Erickson's favorite approaches for changing behavioral patterns. Rosen (1982) provided several examples of how Erickson

reversed a client's pattern to elicit a change in behavior. Two cases are particularly germane to the present discussion:

In the first case, a client sought Erickson's help to lose weight. She weighed 180 pounds but wanted to weigh 130 pounds. The client had many past successes in losing weight, but whenever she reached 130 pounds she would celebrate her success, quickly gaining back the 50 pounds. Erickson told the client that he could help, but that she would not like the solution. Desperate to lose the weight permanently, the client promised to do anything. Erickson told her to gain 20 pounds and that when she weighed an even 200 pounds she could start reducing. At every pound she gained, the client implored Erickson to let her start reducing, but he insisted that she keep her promise and gain to an even 200 pounds if his intervention was to be effective. When the woman reached 200 pounds, she was thrilled to finally begin reducing. When she finally achieved 130 pounds, she never gained the weight back, insisting that she did not want to go through that torture again.

The second case involved Anne, a medical student at Wayne State Medical School, where Erickson was on the faculty. Although a straight-A student, Anne never managed to get to classes on time. She had been lectured by her professors and cursed by her fellow students for holding them up in laboratory work. She would invariably apologize and promise to be on time—all to no avail. The faculty was particularly jubilant when Anne began Erickson's class, since he had a reputation for using drastic tactics on students who wanted to "have it out" with him. In typical fashion, Anne was 20 minutes late to Erickson's first class. Erickson motioned for the students to be quiet and then he graciously, and in an exaggerated fashion, bowed to her. Every student subsequently bowed as Anne made her way to her seat. After class, in the hallway, the dean, custodian, secretary, and everyone that met Anne bowed to her that day. The next day, Anne was the first student in class. Although she easily withstood rebukes from professors, the dean, and fellow students, Anne could not tolerate the silent bowing. She was on time for the rest of the semester.

In the first case, the intervention was successful because Erickson reversed the client's pattern—making her gain, then reduce weight (not reduce, then gain). Once the pattern was broken, the client could no longer go through the sequence

the way she had all her life. Like many people with weight problems, the client had a tolerance level corresponding to a certain weight (180 pounds), at which point she urgently felt the need to reduce. Erickson surpassed the woman's tolerance level by making her gain 20 more pounds.

In the second case, instead of trying to change Anne's behavior through verbal reprimands, Erickson used nonverbal bowing to show Anne that she was using her power in a reverse manner. Erickson was congratulating Anne on her power by bowing—a way of paying homage. Anne realized that she was using her power in a self-hurting manner. When she understood this, she could determine how to use her power constructively.

In both cases, Erickson changed the context surrounding the behaviors. He made no attempt to challenge either behavior directly—an approach that would have certainly created resistance. Also, Erickson believed that the power to change resided

within the individual. This belief is predicated on the assumption that individuals possess the requisite skills for behaving correctly but choose not to because the inappropriate behavior serves an adaptive function. By changing the context, the function, or the purpose, the behavior is changed.

An example of changing the context of behavior in the classroom is the "do-nothing chair" strategy.

The "Do-Nothing Chair" Strategy

The "do-nothing chair" strategy is an effective way to deal with students who are acting passive-aggressively, that is, students who quietly and nondisruptively choose not to follow directions. Here is an example:

A student was given a math worksheet to complete during the last 15 minutes of class. Instead of working on the assignment the student was sitting passively. Let us assume that the passivity was an oppositional way for the student to obtain power and control. The harder the teacher tried to get the student to complete the assignment, the more oppositional he became. The reason was simple: He was being reinforced by the teacher's unsuccessful attempts to get him to comply. The desired outcome of power and control was accomplished by the teacher's frustration.

Here's an alternative approach: The teacher gives the student permission to do nothing. The student is then in a position where opposition becomes cooperation. If the student wants to be oppositional, he must work on his assignment rather than do nothing. Doing nothing is then viewed as being compliant—something that does not accomplish the desired outcome of power and control. You can use this strategy in your own classroom by setting up a "do-nothing chair."

Place a chair in your classroom designated as the "do-nothing chair." Do not use this chair for time-out or place it in a part of the room associated with time-out or any form of punishment. There are two reasons for making this recommendation: First, students could refuse to go to the "do-nothing chair" if it was associated with punishment. This would allow students to obtain power and control. Second, students may view going to the "do-nothing chair" as a "badge of honor," increasing their popularity among certain peers.

When a student passively refuses to complete an assignment, instruct him or her to take a seat in the "do-nothing chair." When the student is in the chair, enthusiastically and genuinely encourage him or her to do nothing—permit him or her to do nothing. It is important not to show anger, irritation, or frustration at the student's passivity. Behavioral displays of these emotions only reinforce passivity by allowing students to obtain power and control. Instead, convey that you are pleased that the student has the opportunity to get even better at doing nothing. Here is an example of how to present the "do-nothing chair":

> "Horace, I see that you are doing nothing instead of working on your math assignment. I've also noticed that you frequently do nothing when given assignments. You certainly are getting good at doing nothing. But, I think you can get even better at doing nothing. And I'm so pleased because I have a chair over there where you can sit and practice getting better at doing nothing. It's the "do-nothing chair." I am confident that you will get better at doing nothing because I have seen how good you have gotten at other tasks at which you practice repeatedly, such as shooting free throws in basketball."

Several elements in this example should be pointed out:

1. By stating to the student what he was doing ("I see that you are doing nothing..."), the teacher has initiated the process of building rapport. The student cannot legitimately argue that he is not doing nothing. To do so would be incongruent with his goal of obtaining power and control through passivity.

2. The teacher was pleased, rather than annoyed, that the student had an opportunity to get even better at "doing nothing." Consequently, the power and control the student may have obtained from frustrating the teacher is eliminated.

3. The teacher linked the idea of practicing "doing nothing" to practicing something the student enjoyed (shooting free throws in basketball). This statement changes the context. "Practicing" was positively recast.

4. A time limit was not placed on sitting in the chair. Placing a time limit would only give the student power and control—he could leave the chair before or after the time was up.

Remember, if the student goes to the "do-nothing chair," he or she is being compliant. When we obtain compliance in one area, it becomes easier to obtain compliance in another area. If the student decides to "do something"—stay in his or her chair, or even argue with us—we can look puzzled and then saddened that the student is giving up a wonderful opportunity to become good at "doing nothing." Because staying in the chair or arguing is "doing something," it then becomes easier for us to get another, more posi-

tive behavior. We often find passivity more difficult to deal with than overt misbehavior because when the student is passive he or she is giving us nothing to react to. Getting the student to "do something" makes the behavior easier to manage.

Whatever the student chooses to do—work on the assignment, move to the "do-nothing chair," stay in his or her seat and do nothing, or argue, the context surrounding the behavior is still changed. The misbehavior no longer angers us. "Doing nothing" is permitted and encouraged, but restricted to a certain location.

There are several common concerns educators voice about the "do-nothing chair" strategy. Sometimes we are reluctant to tell students to "do nothing" because that direction conflicts with the goals of education. However, if a student is "doing nothing" anyway, and our best traditional efforts have failed, then we have nothing to lose—and potentially a lot to gain—by permitting the student's behavior, but changing the context. In addition, "doing nothing" then comes under our control, rather than our student's control.

Another common concern is that the student will refuse to move and still refuse to do anything. If the student refuses to go to the "do-nothing chair" but also refuses to do anything, simply point out that the "do-nothing chair" floats around the room, and now the student is in it.

The third common concern is how to deal with a student who goes to the "do-nothing chair" but begins doing something, such as making animal noises or doodling. In the case of making animal noises, we can simply inform the student that he or she is now sitting in the "animal-noise chair." Remember that compliance has already been obtained—the student moved to the chair—so it is easier to obtain compliance in another area. Also, if the student is making animal noises, then he or she is "doing something." When a student is "doing something"—even if the behavior is inappropriate—it becomes easier to get the student to do something else that is more appropriate.

In the case of a student doodling, we can remind the student that he or she is in the "do-nothing chair." Nonchalantly remove any writing material, remind the student that this is a chance to get really good at doing nothing, and explain that you would not want any materials to interfere. Alternatively, if the student is doodling, then he or she is "doing something".... The point is that we need to take whatever our students give us, meeting them in their frames of reference and proceeding from there, rather than trying to fit their behaviors into our concepts of how they should act.

If the "do-nothing chair" is to be effective, we must consider the purpose of the student's passive behavior (obtaining power and control). If the desired outcome for "doing nothing" is power and control, then the "do-nothing chair" will work when properly implemented. On the other hand, if the desired outcome for "doing nothing" is avoidance of a task, then the "do-nothing chair" strategy will be ineffective because the student will accomplish the desired outcome of avoiding a task perceived as boring, irrelevant, or too difficult. If the desired outcome is attention from peers, then it's essential that the "do-nothing chair" be implemented in a way that it is not perceived as a "badge of honor."

Chapter 9

Consequent Manipulations

The previous section focused on **antecedent manipulations**—things we can do to alter the events that come *before*, and often trigger or cue, a behavior. In this section, three approaches are described which focus on **consequent manipulations**—changing the environment *after* behavior occurs to promote compliance.

Most people hold the colloquial view that "consequences" is synonymous with "punishment" and that "punishment" is synonymous with "discipline." Reinforcement and rewards are not typically thought of as consequences. In reality, "consequences" refers to anything that occurs after a behavior is performed. It is important to understand these functional definitions if we are to use consequent manipulations effectively to manage resistance.

We often wrongly assume that *discipline* and *punishment* are synonymous. A quick glance at the disciplinary practices that appear in the "Policies and Procedures Handbook" of most schools reveals an almost exclusive focus on punishment: in-school and out-of-school suspensions, expulsion, fines, detention, restitution, and, in some states, even corporal punishment. Yet, according to the *American Heritage Dictionary*, **discipline** refers to "training that is expected to produce a specific character or pattern of behavior, especially training that produces moral or mental improvement." A key word in this definition is *improvement*. In contrast to discipline, *punishment* does one thing: It decreases a behavior. Suppressing a student's inappropriate behavior with punishment does not guarantee that the student knows the appropriate replacement behavior. There is a perverse irony when we evoke punishment with the phrase "I'm going to teach you a lesson." Teaching involves giving students skills and knowledge, not suppressing or eliminating behavior. Therefore, *discipline* has more in common with *positive reinforcement*, which increases behavior, than it does with *punishment*.

In order to understand discipline better, it is helpful to examine the concepts of positive reinforcement and punishment more thoroughly. **Positive**

reinforcement *increases* the probability the behavior it follows reoccurs in the future. **Punishment** *decreases* the probability the behavior it follows reoccurs in the future. The key consideration in these two definitions is that positive reinforcement and punishment are not *things* that are received or removed, but rather *effects*. The following examples may further clarify that positive reinforcement and punishment are effects.

A student is yelling excessively and running around a classroom. As a *consequence*, the teacher spends a few minutes talking "understandingly" with the student—conveying warmth and caring, empathy, and unconditional, positive regard for the precipitating circumstances in the student's life. As a result of this communication, the student stops yelling and running. By definition, the teacher's attention was *punishment* because its effect was a *decrease* in unwanted behaviors.

The opposite effect can also occur. For example, as a *consequence* for placing her hand too close to a hot burner, a parent may sternly say "no" and slap the back of the toddler's hand. This action may create pain and even temporary reddening of the skin. Yet, if the toddler repeatedly places her hand by the burner for several ensuing days, then the slap was not *punishment*. It was *positive reinforcement* because its effect was an *increase* in the behavior. We sometimes look upon students who continue to behave poorly even after being punished as disordered or as displaying masochistic tendencies. We fail to understand that the attention they receive from us may be more reinforcing than the pain inflicted from the punishment.

The preceding two examples illustrate the functional definitions of *punishment* and *positive reinforcement* as based on their effect on behavior. These definitions are often misunderstood because of the colloquial way in which they are viewed. In the second example, the common assumption made is that punishment was the "thing" administered—the physical slap—not its effect. If punishment is effective, it is used less rather than more frequently because the inappropriate behavior is decreasing until it is eliminated. When we *repeatedly* give students verbal reprimands, send them out of the classroom, or give them suspensions, we are not punishing them. We are administering positive reinforcement. The adage "negative attention is better than no attention" certainly applies here. We expect students to behave well, and ignore them when they do so. But we usually give students negative attention when they behave poorly. Our attention, even if it is negative, is a powerful reinforcer—especially for students with the most challenging behaviors who typically receive very little positive attention. In essence, negative attention is a surefire way to give these students the power and control that they so desperately want.

The distinction between form and function is not well understood when applied to the use of punishment. **Form** is how a behavior is displayed (i.e., what it looks like). **Function** is the purpose the behavior serves (i.e., what goal/outcome the student obtains from performing the behavior).

Here is a telling example: A teacher was disturbed that a student frequently did not bring her reading book to class. As a consequence, the teacher required the student to write 100 times "I will remember my book."

Most of us would probably view this consequence as *punishment*. Yet, when we consider the functional definition of punishment as an effect—a decrease in behavior—we must ask, what behavior was the teacher trying to decrease—remembering the book? This case illustrates how we misunderstand and misapply punishment—with

The common use of the term positive reinforcement causes similar difficulties. Some educators see positive reinforcement as a manipulative tool created to coerce students into behaving appropriately. Viewed as bribery, positive reinforcement is seen as undermining students' abilities to become self-directed and intrinsically motivated.

The major reasons for this misunderstanding is the equating of the term *positive reinforcement* with reward. Unlike reinforcement, a reward is a *thing* given to acknowledge an accomplishment. Synonyms for reward are "merit" or "prize." In real life, rewards may or may not function as reinforcers. For example, an athlete may begin training to compete in the discus throw several years before the summer Olympic games. During this time, his discus-throwing behavior would occur at a high rate as part of his training. His effort pays off and he wins the Olympic Gold Medal—certainly the ultimate *reward*—and decides to retire from competition. The subsequent frequency of his discus-throwing behavior decreases. Therefore, the reward (the Olympic Gold Medal) functioned as *punishment* since its effect was to *decrease* discus-throwing behavior. If the athlete places a disappointing 10th and subsequently spends more time practicing throwing the discus to compete more effectively in the next Olympiad, then his poor showing functioned as *reinforcement* since it had the effect of increasing his discus-throwing behavior.

These examples are difficult for us to comprehend because they challenge the popular views of reinforcement and punishment. Many educators are

counterproductive results. When we first try to define the purpose of the student's behavior, we learn that the student has a reading disability and was embarrassed about this problem. Therefore, "forgetting" to bring the book to class served the *function* of avoiding being embarrassed in front of peers for having to read books at a lower reading level.

There are many simple ways the teacher could have dealt with this student's embarrassment:

- Have the student sit in the back of the class where other students can't easily see her book.

- Have all students cover their reading books in brown paper-bag book covers.

- Use books that are modified for struggling readers but still appear to be grade-level books.

- Ask the student what can be done to help her not feel embarrassed.

puzzled as to how talking nicely to a student, for example, could be punishment because they believe punishment must certainly be something unpleasant. However, once we understand that reinforcement and punishment are *effects* rather than *things*, our ability to manage noncompliant behaviors increases dramatically.

Choosing Effective Reinforcers

The use of reinforcement to manage resistance is deceptively straightforward: Reinforce the student for performing compliance behaviors. Rhode, Jenson, and Reavis (1992) described a novel approach for using reinforcement to engender compliance. This technique, called the Compliance Matrix, is a variation of Bingo—a popular game in which players use matrix cards to win prizes. The word *matrix* refers to a square composed of several equal-sized cells. To implement the Compliance Matrix you'll need:

- Several matrices with numbered cells such as those appearing in *Figure 3-6* and in the Reproducibles section.

- Cardboard key tags, available from office supply stores, or small pink erasers, poker chips, checkers, or slips of paper. Label each object with a number from the matrix. Include one marked "Wild Card.")

- An opaque container to hold the numbered objects.

To implement this technique, Matrix X (see *Figure 3-6* and Reproducibles section) is posted or drawn on the blackboard in an area visible to the target student. The numbered objects (e.g., key tags) are placed in the opaque container. When a student complies with requests, is following classroom rules, or is on-task working he or she gets to draw an object. When an object is drawn, the corresponding number on the matrix is marked with an "X." If the student draws the Wild Card, he or she can pick any number to be marked off on the matrix.

The student earns a pre-selected reinforcer (a discussion of reinforcers follows) after any row, column, or diagonal is completed on the matrix. The matrix board is then erased and the game starts over. Matrix Y is introduced after the student is

---

Winning Compliance Matrices

Matrix X

X	2	3
A	5	6
X	8	9

Matrix Y

X	2	3	4
5	6	7	8
9	10	11	12
13	14	15	16

Matrix Z

1	2	3	4	5
6	7	8	9	10
11	12	13	14	15
16	17	18	19	20
21	22	23	24	25

Figure 3-6

Note. From *The Tough Kid Book* (p.84) Rhode, G; Jenson, W; and Reavis, K, 1992, Longmont, CO: Sopris West. Reprinted with permission.

responding to your directives at a high rate. Matrix Z is introduced when a high rate of compliance achieved with Matrix Y.

Rather than targeting one student, Rhode et al. (1992) described two ways the Compliance Matrix can be used to promote compliance with groups of students. When used with either a single target student or with groups, the Compliance Matrix, reinforcers, and the opaque container are placed in the front of the room. The predetermined reinforcer, or Mystery Motivator, is posted next to the matrix to build class expectations. Students who follow a directive are randomly chosen to select one of the numbered objects. When a row, column, or diagonal is completed, the entire class receives the reinforcer.

The second modification for group use involves splitting the class into several teams. Each team is assigned a color and the team's color can be marked in the matrix cell of the drawn number whenever a student of that team complies with the teacher's requests. Several teams can occupy the same cell if they randomly draw that cell's number. This approach encourages teams to compete at being compliant and following classroom rules. Any number of teams can win by reaching the set criterion. A student who tries to sabotage his or her team's effort can be made a one-person team.

Reinforcement Programs

In order for the Compliance Matrix to be effective, we need to deliver reinforcement. Rhode et al. (1992) described several effective reinforcement programs: Chart Moves, Mystery Motivators, and Spinners. An additional reinforcement program is the 49 Square Chart (Jenson, Andrews, and Reavis, 1992).

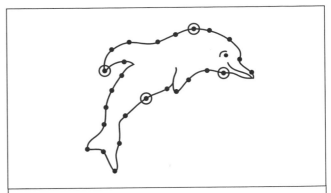

Figure 3-7
A completed dot-to-dot picture used in the Chart Moves reinforcement program.

Chart Moves

In Chart Moves, students connect one of the dots in a dot-to-dot picture when they perform compliance-based behaviors. *Figure 3-7* provides an example of a completed dot-to-dot picture. A blank master is also included in the Reproducibles section.

There are a variety of ways to administer Chart Moves. First, you can have students select from several available dot-to-dot pictures and then earn chances to connect the dots by performing prespecified, compliance-based behaviors. In this case, the finished picture would show the reinforcer earned. The second way to administer Chart Moves is to have students select reinforcers— either trinkets or slips of paper with privileges written on them—from a bag once the dot-to-dot picture is complete. In this case, the dots provide students with a visual representation of how close they are getting to earning the reinforcer. In both Chart Moves approaches, "special dots" can be created by circling them. Interspersing these "special dots" throughout the picture provides more frequent access to reinforcement. When students connect to one of the "special dots" they receive small reinforcers. At the end, they receive a bigger one.

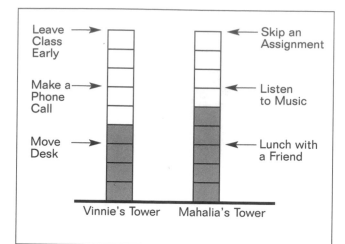

Figure 3-8
Example of Towers used in Chart Moves
Note. Adapted from *The Tough Kid Book* (p.44), Rhode, G.; Jenson, W., and Reavis, K., 1992, Longmont, CO: Sopris West. Reprinted with permission.

Middle and high school students may find dot-to-dot pictures too "babyish." For these students, try having them create towers (see *Figure 3-8*). Students shade in one increment each time they engage in the requested behavior. When a student reaches a designated level, he or she earns the specified reinforcer. This approach can also be modified by letting students select a reinforcer from a menu or grab bag when they reach a designated level.

Mystery Motivators

The first step in using a Mystery Motivator is to generate a list of positive reinforcers with input from your students. Write down the reinforcers on slips of paper and place each slip in an individual envelope. Display the envelopes in a prominent place for all your students to see or have students decorate the sealed envelopes and place them inside a shoe box. Then take a calendar and place pieces of opaque tape or small Post-It® notes over each school day for the entire year. As students perform target compliance behaviors, they earn the right to uncover that day on the calendar. If

an "X" appears, the student can open the Mystery Motivator envelope and obtain the reinforcer. The number of "Xs" you write on the calendar determines the frequency with which students receive reinforcement.

Spinners

You can modify a spinner from a board game or make one out of cardboard. Divide the spinner into five or more sections (see *Figure 3-9*). In each section draw a picture of the reinforcer or write its name. When a student performs a target compliance-based behavior, he or she takes a spin. Whichever section the arrow lands on is the reinforcer that is obtained.

A variation of this approach is to write the numbers one through five on the sections of the spinner as depicted in *Figure 3-10*. When a student follows your direction, he or she earns a spin. A grab-bag can be made for each number, filled with trinkets and slips of paper with privileges written on them. When the spinner lands on a number,

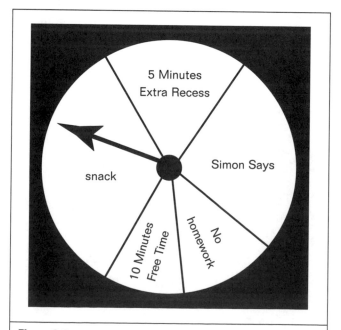

Figure 3-9
A spinner with reinforcers.

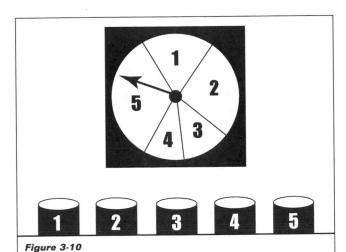

Figure 3-10
A numbered spinner with accompanying grab-bags of reinforcers.

the student randomly draws from the grab-bag that corresponds to the number.

There are numerous other variations that can be devised using spinners. Students can earn tokens when they engage in the requested behavior. The number of tokens represents the number of times the student can spin the spinner. This adds novelty to the intervention. Some teachers get even more elaborate. The numbers on the spinner can represent points that students can accumulate (e.g., if a student spins a three, he or she receives three points). Students can then exchange points at a designated time for privileges and activities. In another variation, students only get to spin and earn points when they perform the targeted behavior. Only after reaching a specified number of points can the student select a reinforcer from a grab-bag.

49 Square Chart

Create a 49 Square Chart by dividing two poster boards into 49 squares of equal size using a ruler and permanent marker (see *Figure 3-11*). Laminate one of the poster boards—this will be the 49 Square Chart. Cut out the other board's squares. Fasten these squares to the top of each

square on the chart with velcro fasteners or masking tape so that they can be peeled off to reveal the square below.

Randomly mark an "X" in several of the boxes throughout the chart and apply the square covers. When a student performs the requested behavior, he or she earns the privilege of removing a cover to see if an "X" is designated below. If an "X" appears, then the entire group wins a reinforcer, such as a popcorn party or video viewing.

The number of "X"s that appear on the chart can be decreased over time so that students are working to earn a chance at a relatively obscure reinforcer. However, it is important not to decrease the number of "X"s too quickly, otherwise students will not find this program reinforcing.

You might administer the 49 Square Chart so that the reinforcer is won by an individual student instead of the group. In either case, you can also try these variations:

49 Square Chart						
1	2	3	4	5	6	7
8	9	10	11	12	13	14
15	16	17	18	19	20	21
22	23	24	25	26	27	28
29	30	31	32	33	34	35
36	37	38	39	40	41	42
43	44	45	46	47	48	49

Figure 3-11
An example of how to set up a 49 Square Chart.

1. Students need to earn a specific number of points in order to obtain the privilege of removing a cover. For example, you might set the criterion at 10 points. When any student earns 10 points, he or she takes a turn uncovering one of the squares.

2. Alternatively, determine a specific number of squares with an "X" that must be uncovered before a student or group earns the reinforcer. For example, a criteria of five "X"s could be required before a reinforcer is earned. In this variation, students who perform the target behavior would either take a turn uncovering a square or they would be required to earn a certain number of points before they can uncover a square. In either arrangement, a certain number of "X"s must be uncovered before a student or group has access to the reinforcer.

Reinforcement Is Individual

At the beginning of this section the statement was made that using reinforcement is deceptively straightforward. The approach is *straightforward* because we are simply reinforcing compliance. The approach is deceptive because is it not easy to find effective reinforcers. The principal consideration for finding effective reinforcers is understanding that reinforcement is *individual*. What one student finds reinforcing, another may find punishing. The most effective way to determine which reinforcers your students find reinforcing is observing what they like to do when they are given free access to materials or activities. This approach is based on the idea of making problem behavior work for us.

Let us imagine being children again on the first occasion when our parents left us home alone. Let us think of the activities we engaged in when our parents were gone. Here are some possibilities:

1. Eat junk food

2. Torture younger siblings

3. Play music loudly

4. Make crank phone calls

5. Watch restricted TV programs

6. Snoop in parent's things

7. Bounce on furniture

This list is not meant to be exhaustive, but rather illustrative. Here is another list of possible activities. How many of us would say that we engaged in any of these while our parents were away from the house?

1. Watch news or a documentary on TV

2. Do yard work

3. Eat a can of vegetables

4. Vacuum the carpet

5. Cook dinner for the family

6. Do laundry

7. Dust furniture

When we were free to do whatever we wanted while our parents were gone, certain behaviors had a higher probability of occurring than others. These high probability behaviors are the most powerful reinforcers. In the classroom we can generate a list of powerful reinforcers by observing what students do when they are free to select materials or activities.

This approach makes use of the Premack principle—making high probability behaviors contingent on low probability behaviors (Premack, 1959). Here's another example of a strategy using the Premack principle:

In 1963, Lloyd Homme had the task of controlling the behavior of three three-year-olds without using punishment or tangible reinforcers, such as candy or trinkets. One child was screaming and running around the room. Another was noisily pushing a chair across the floor. A third was playing with a puzzle. Homme simply made participation in these behaviors contingent on the children doing a small amount—very small at first—of what he wanted them to do. His first request was that they sit quietly in chairs and look at the blackboard. This direction was followed by the command, "Everybody run and scream now." (Levitt and Rutherford, 1978).

This contingency, based on the Premack principle, gave Homme immediate control over the children's behavior.

Sometimes the Premack principle is called "Mom's Rule" because many parents use access to high probability behaviors as reinforcers for the occurrence of low probability behaviors. For example, many mothers tell their children, "After you finish your spinach you can have a bowl of ice cream."

In addition to observing the behaviors of students during free access situations, we can observe which behaviors they engage in frequently. For example, we might observe that many junior high school students spend an inordinate amount of class time writing notes to their friends. Therefore, note writing may be a powerful reinforcer. In this situation, you might tell a student

that after she finishes her math assignment, she can write a note to a friend. If her performance on the assignment reaches a specified criterion, you might also allow her to deliver the note to her friend.

Many problem behaviors students exhibit can be used as reinforcers—providing they are not dangerous to self or others and do not interfere with anyone's ability to learn. In this way we ensure that we have effective reinforcers.

Here is an example from my own work with a seventh-grade boy (Maag, 1996):

He was having great difficulty getting homework assignments completed in his history class. In addition, he was regularly reprimanded by his teacher for talking during class and mumbling under his breath when the teacher brought these behaviors to his attention. The teacher had met with the parents and had implored them to get their son to finish his assignments and improve his attitude in class. Having little success, the parents brought their son to see me. Among other things, the boy related a fairly strong distaste for his history teacher. He had no trouble discussing at great length the personal and professional shortcomings of his teacher. This strong distaste gave me an idea. The junior high schools in town were sponsoring a carnival on Saturday, two weeks from my meeting with the boy. One of the carnival games was "dunk the teacher." A staple at carnivals, this game involves having a person sit on a chair while patrons take turns throwing balls at a bullseye. When a ball hits the bullseye, the person falls into a tank of water. It is great fun for everybody.

After the family left my office, I called the school and asked to talk to the boy's history teacher. After he explained the problems to me, I told him I thought I had a way to increase the boy's assignment completion and appropriate behavior in class. In turn, I would require a "small" favor of him. I asked him if he would be willing to sit in the dunking chair for one of the half-hour time slots. There was a pause and then he asked why. I explained that I wanted to use him as a reinforcer to increase the boy's assignment completion and behavior in class. I explained how the boy seemed to have some negative feelings toward him and that I thought the boy would work well for the opportunity to dunk him in water. He somewhat skeptically agreed.

At my next session, I presented the boy with the opportunity to dunk his history teacher. His eyes immediately lighted up but then asked, "What's the catch?"

"The catch is," I replied, "that you must complete your assignments and improve your behavior in his class." I went on to explain exactly what "improved behavior" meant. I also told the boy that every time he completed an assignment, he would receive one ticket for the carnival. After further conferring with the teacher, I told the boy he would also receive one ticket for every 10 minutes in class he was being polite and attentive. I reminded him that three throws at this carnival game equaled three tickets. Therefore, he could potentially earn about 30 chances to dunk his

teacher. Needless to say, the boy was very excited about the prospect of being able to dunk his teacher. As a result, his assignment completion and classroom behavior improved dramatically (pp. 63-64).

Note. From *Parenting Without Punishment* (pp. 63-64) by Maag, J., 1996, Philadelphia: Charles Press. Reprinted with permission.

Not only did this student's behavior improve, it also remained improved after the carnival. Because he experienced this reinforcer, it became easier for the student to identify other, more readily available, reinforcers.

By permitting students to engage in problem behaviors, contingent upon completing requested behaviors, we change the context surrounding the problem behavior. The problem behaviors then eventually lose their reinforcing value. We can then begin to use more traditional activities and privileges as reinforcers. Following are two examples illustrating the use of problem behaviors as effective reinforcers and their subsequent loss of reinforcing value.

A 12-year-old student identified as behaviorally disordered was attending a day treatment program through the local school district. He displayed several challenging behaviors, including swearing and never finishing assignments. Staff efforts to get the student to stop swearing and complete assignments met with much resistance. By swearing, the student obtained power, control, and status. In fact, the higher the perceived status of a staff member, the more he seemed to enjoy swearing. He enjoyed swearing at administrators the most. He would even sneak into the administrators' offices and begin swearing. The student also obtained power and control by not completing assignments. No one could make him do what he did not want to do.

The intervention was straightforward. If the student completed four out of five assignments during the week (never five out of five because that would set him up for failure), the student would be allowed to spend 10 minutes swearing at the principal on Friday. (The principal agreed to participate in this intervention because, while she did not approve of students swearing, she was not personally offended by it, having worked with students with behavioral disorders for many years.) The student enthusiastically and correctly completed all his assignments. On Friday, he eagerly entered the principal's office. She came around the front of her desk and sat in a chair, motioning for the boy to sit in the other chair. He preferred to stand and, while pointing a finger at her, proceeded to say, "You… you… you… YOU!" He then walked out, without swearing a single time.

In this example, the problem behavior (swearing) was used to reinforce assignment completion. The student initially wanted to swear at the principal. But when swearing was permitted, it lost its power and control value. Of course, the student's desire for power and control did not vanish. Swearing simply no longer served this function. He would need to be taught a replacement behavior—an appropriate way to obtain power and control—in order for this intervention to result in long-lasting behavior change. Because swearing was no longer reinforcing, the staff could introduce more traditional reinforcers, such as privileges and activities.

The second example of using problem behaviors as reinforcers involves a therapist working with a 16-year-old boy who was depressed:

> The chief complaint of the boy's parents was that their son isolated himself in his room the minute he came home from school. He would only come out briefly to nibble at food during dinner and then immediately retreat to his room. The more the parents tried to coax him out of his room, the more resistant the boy became to leaving his room. His parents even threatened to remove his bedroom door.

It is not difficult to determine what two functions "isolating" serves for an adolescent who is depressed. First, "isolating" served the purpose of escape and avoidance. Individuals who are depressed often view interactions with others—and life in general—as aversive and want to escape. Second, by resisting his parents' attempts to get him to leave his room, the boy obtained a degree of power and control—a very important outcome for individuals who are depressed. One of the major characteristics of depression are feelings of helplessness. Exerting power and control by refusing to come out of his room helped the boy fight these feelings.

The intervention was straightforward:

> If the boy would play a board game with his parents for 10 minutes after dinner, then he had permission to isolate in his room. If he stayed out of his room for 15 minutes or more, interacting with family, then when he returned to his room, his parents were to bang on his door, frantically pleading with him to come out.

Permitting the boy to isolate in his room started off as a powerful reinforcer for playing a game with his parents. But "isolating" began to lose its reinforcing value when the parents permitted it. By having the boy play a game, the parents exposed him to pleasurable interactions with others which would become reinforcing in and of themselves.

The context, meaning, purpose, and subsequent desire to isolate were also changed by the parents' desperate pleading for the boy to come out of his room after he earned the right to isolate. The boy could see how silly isolating was when his parents gave him what he wanted—power and control—by pleading for him to come out of his room.

In this example, the boy was reinforced by being able to go to his room after interacting with his family for short periods of time. However, the context was changed in two ways. First, he was given permission to isolate in his room, whereas before the parents were pleading for him to come out. Second, his parents would bang on his door (as before), but only after he stayed out of his room for a period of time. The power and control value was removed because the parents now enjoyed banging on their son's door because he had stayed out of his room for a period of time.

Avoiding Reinforcement Burn-Out

To be effective, we must have a large supply of reinforcers from which students can choose. It is common to be excited at the initial success of an intervention, only to find two weeks later that it no longer works. A common reaction is, "I guess reinforcement only works for a short period of time." Reinforcement will work forever. However, reinforcers can lose their effectiveness over time. In essence, students burn out on too much of one thing. The technical term for this phenomenon is **satiation**. When students experience a reinforcer

to such an extent that it is no longer reinforcing, satiation has been reached. You can prevent satiation by limiting access to the reinforcer or by giving a small amount of the reinforcer. You can also prevent satiation by having a large number of potential reinforcers from which students can choose. This practice reduces the chances of burn out on any one privilege or activity. The previously described reinforcement programs require collecting a fairly large number of potential reinforcers.

Reinforcers not only lose effectiveness. In some cases, what was once reinforcing to a student can actually become punishing. This can happen to us even as adults. Many adults dislike bologna sandwiches because of the tremendous amount of bologna they consumed as children. Some adults have an aversion to particular types of alcohol because of an experience in young adulthood that led to a terrible hangover.

Another example of how a reinforcer can become a punishment is the case of a strategy used in the 1970s and early 1980s to get people to stop smoking. Although its long-term success is questionable, the approach is illustrative. Clients would go to the clinic and sit at a table with an ashtray and cigarettes. They would be instructed to smoke as many cigarettes as quickly as possible within a certain period of time. Satiation readily occurred.

Although the passage of time can lessen the effects of satiation, the best defense against its occurrence is to have a large supply of privileges and activities your students will find reinforcing.

Reducing Competing Sources of Reinforcement

Some students resist following our directions when their inappropriate behaviors are reinforced by peers. For example, a student who makes an animal noise in class may be reinforced by peers in the form of smiles, giggles, and eye contact. Even negative comments from peers (e.g., "Gross," "Stop it, you moron!" "Grow up!") can be highly reinforcing because the student obtains attention and perhaps power and control. Two common approaches to dealing with inappropriate behavior are ignoring the behavior and punishing the student. Neither one of these approaches is successful when the student is receiving reinforcement from peers. It is professionally irresponsible to punish a student for a behavior while allowing the reinforcement to continue. Reinforcement is strong. It will win out over punishment unless the punishment is severe. For example, the student making animal noises may be punished by having to stay after school, having a teacher-parent conference, and having her parents take away television-watching privileges. The student may indeed find these consequences aversive. However, receiving the attention from peers is more powerful than the negative consequences. For an intervention to work in this case, it must focus on the peer group as well as the student. One approach is to reinforce peers for ignoring the student when she makes animal noises. Another approach is to use one of two types of group-oriented contingencies: dependent and interdependent.

Reinforcing Peers

When a student behaves inappropriately (e.g., making animal noises in class), scan the room and note which peers provide the most attention to the student for displaying the behavior. Peers may have either looked at the student or made com-

ments. Note both the positive and negative comments made to the student. Both types of comments can be equally reinforcing. Positive comments (i.e., those that encourage the student to make more animal noises) allow the student to obtain attention from peers. Negative comments (i.e., those that are critical of the student making animal noises) permit the student to obtain power and control over those peers by getting reactions from them. Sometimes the student receives the most attention from those who sit the closest. In other instances, the most attention may come from very vocal peers.

Write down the names of the peers who provide the most attention (verbal and nonverbal). Then individually discuss with each peer that giving the student attention for inappropriate behavior interrupts the lesson and results in lost time that must be made up after school. Explain that losing lesson time can be avoided by not providing attention to the student. Also tell the peers that you have their names on a piece of paper readily available during the lesson.

During class, any time the target student exhibits the inappropriate behavior, quickly look at the peers. Make a tally mark beside the names of

Reinforcers	Tally Marks Needed
Helping the coach	30 tally marks
Decorating bulletin board	30 tally marks
Reading a story out loud to a classmate	30 tally marks
Listening to music	20 tally marks
Passing a note to a friend	20 tally marks
Going to Library	15 tally marks
Playing "Go Fish"	15 tally marks
Art time	10 tally marks
Show and Tell	10 tally marks
Borrowing a book	5 tally marks
Erasing the blackboard	5 tally marks

Figure 3-12
An example of a student-generated list of reinforcers used in peer reinforcement.

peers who are *not* looking or talking to the student. Record two tally marks whenever a peer does look at or talk to the student (i.e., gives

attention) when the student is working on-task. At the end of the lesson, inform the peers of the number of tally marks they earned. Let them

The Good Behavior Game

Materials Needed: Large glass jar, marbles, beeper tape, tape player, electrical tape

Implementation Steps:

1. Write three appropriate behaviors (e.g., eyes on teacher, feet on floor, raise hand before talking) on the left side of the blackboard.

2. Write three inappropriate behaviors (e.g., talking to a neighbor, throwing stuff, out of seat) on the right side of the blackboard.

3. Above the appropriate behaviors write "+3 Points." Above the inappropriate behaviors write "-1 Point." *Figure 3-13* shows how this would appear on the blackboard.

4. In the front of the room, set up the glass jar with a line of electrical tape wrapped around it, marbles, and tape player with the beeper tape. (To create a beeper tape, refer to the Reproducibles section).

5. Explain to your students that whenever the tape beeps, if everyone is performing one of the three appropriate behaviors, three marbles will be placed in the jar. However, if anyone is engaging in any of the three inappropriate behaviors, one marble will be removed from the jar. Just one marble should be removed (not one for each inappropriate behavior). This ratio sets up students for success by allowing them to earn more marbles than they can lose.

6. Ten minutes before the end of class, check the jar. If the jar is filled with marbles to the line, each student gets to select one of several free-time activities in which to engage during the last 10 minutes of class.

Modifications:

You can make modifications as you see fit when implementing the Good Behavior Game. Here are some ideas:

1. Instead of marbles, use candy. At then end of class if the jar is filled to the line, pass out the candy equally to everyone in class. As an added incentive, designate the last five minutes of class as time when students can trade candy with each other. (Be sure to check with parents before implementing this modification in case any students have dietary restrictions.)

2. Instead of using a jar and marbles, simply keep track of the number of points the class earns by making tally marks on the blackboard. You'll still need a predetermined number of points the class must earn to obtain the reward.

3. Create between 2–4 groups of students. Give each group their own jar. Then when the beep sounds, drop marbles into the jars of each group in which all members are appropriately engaged. Take out one marble from each group jar in which a student is engaged. All the groups that fill their jar to the line before the last 10 minutes of class earn the reward. Alternatively, set up the game so that only the group with the most marbles obtains the reward.

4. Write each student's name on a slip of paper and place it in a bag. Pull one name out of the bag without telling the students whose name was drawn. When the tape beeps, see whether or not that student is engaged in a "+3" behavior or a "-1" behavior and place or remove marbles accordingly. You can either announce the student's name after each beep or keep the names anonymous.

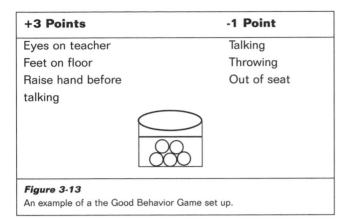

+3 Points	-1 Point
Eyes on teacher	Talking
Feet on floor	Throwing
Raise hand before talking	Out of seat

Figure 3-13
An example of a the Good Behavior Game set up.

"purchase" an activity or privilege with their tally marks from a list of reinforcers (see *Figure 3-12*) and allow them to engage in the activity during the last 10 minutes of class.

The list of activities and privileges in *Figure 3-12* are simply illustrative. In order for the list to be truly reinforcing, enlist the help of your students to generate the list. Then have them rank-order them. Rank-ordering provides an accurate "cost"—the number of tally marks required to earn the activity or privilege. The list can also be individualized to each peer's ranking. This technique employs peers in delivering reinforcement to the student for behaving appropriately. The rationale is straightforward. The student is misbehaving in order to receive attention from peers, so we reinforce peers who provide the student with attention when he or she is behaving appropriately and who ignore the student when he or she is behaving inappropriately. There are two additional ways we can enlist the help of peers and provide the student with power and control for behaving well. Both are group-oriented contingencies.

Using Group-Oriented Contingencies

Most of us recognize the existence of peer pressure in our classrooms, but rarely do we use it to our advantage. In **group-oriented contingency** the entire class is reinforced based on the behav-ior of one student, a number of students, or the entire class. We can develop group-oriented contingencies to minimize the effect of negative peer pressure (e.g., a student receiving peer attention for making animal noises) and maximize the influence of positive peer pressure, encouraging achievement and compliant behavior. There are two type of group-oriented contingencies that are particularly effective when a student's inappropriate behavior is reinforced by obtaining attention, power, or control from peers: dependent group-oriented contingency and interdependent group-oriented contingency (Maag, 1999).

In **dependent group-oriented contingency** reinforcement of the entire group is contingent upon one student's behavior. This approach is sometimes called the "Hero Procedure" because the student earning the reinforcer for the entire group becomes a hero.

To implement a dependent group-oriented contingency, first generate a list of effective reinforcers. Then tell the target student that for every five minutes that she can refrain from the inappropriate behavior (making animal noises), three tally marks will be written on the blackboard. If there are 20 tally marks on the blackboard by the end of the 50-minute class period, the entire class will earn a reward. The reinforcer can be determined using the Spinner or 49 Square Chart strategies described previously. The number of required tally marks depends on the length of your lesson. For example, in a 15-minute lesson it is only possible for the student to earn 9 tally marks.

A variation of this approach utilizes a beeper tape with random tones (see Reproducibles section for instructions on how to create a beeper tape). If the student is not making animal noises when the tape beeps, three points are written on the blackboard. The advantage of using the beeper

Strategies for Reducing Scapegoating	
Strategy	**Description**
Keep the target student's name anonymous.	Place the names of students into a bag. The behavior or performance of the student whose name is drawn determines whether the group earns the reward. The name of the student remains anonymous.
Adjust the criterion for the group-oriented contingency.	Set the criterion at a level so that one student's performance will not prevent the group from receiving the reward. A criterion of an 80% average for the group would allow some students to score below this average without jeopardizing the reward.
Increase the criterion for students who are scapegoating.	Set a higher criterion for students who scapegoat others. For example, require them to obtain a score of 95% correct on an assignment that other students only need to score 85% on. The group can then only earn the reward if the student who is scapegoating gets 95% correct.
Reinforce students who do not engage in scapegoating.	Add 1 point to the score of students who refrain from scapegoating. When selecting one of their names, give them more leeway so that they can score lower and still earn a reward for the class. Or, individual students who refrain from scapegoating can earn several minutes more free time than is specified in the original group reward. Implement a response cost for students who are scapegoating.
Implement a response cost for students who are scapegoating.	Students lose one minute of participating in the group reward for every incident of scapegoating in which they engage while the contingency is in effect.

Table 3-2

tape is that the student does not know when the tape will beep. This increases his or her motivation to refrain from making animal noises in an attempt to earn the maximum number of tally marks possible. The disadvantage is that the student may try to make animal noises between the beeps.

In **interdependent group-oriented contingency** all members of the class are required to refrain from making animal noises (or whatever the target behavior may be) in order for the entire class to earn a reinforcer. Implementing an interdependent group-oriented contingency is the same as dependent group-oriented contingency except that everyone must refrain from making animal noises.

A particularly effective interdependent group-oriented contingency is the Good Behavior Game (Maag, 1999). For the Good Behavior Game to be effective, it is essential to catch your students

being good. Be sure to set them up for success. The first several times you implement this technique, it's important that the marbles reach the line and your students obtain the reward. To determine how many marbles must be earned, multiply the number of beeps on the tape by three (three marbles). This will give you the total number of marbles it is possible for the students to earn. Then decide what the success rate should be. An initial criteria of 70 percent is a good place to start. Multiply the percentage by the total possible marbles. This number is the number of marbles students need to earn in order to receive the reinforcer. For example, let us assume there are 30 beeps on the tape. That means the most marbles the class can earn is 90 (30 x 3 = 90). If we set the initial criterion at 70 percent, the total number of marbles the class would need to earn would be 63 (.70 x 90 = 63). Place 63 marbles into the jar and wrap black electrical tape around the jar even with the top level of the marbles. Once students have experienced success raise the criterion. Keep in mind that the jar will need to be big enough to accommodate more marbles when you increase the criterion and move the tape higher. Regardless of how much you increase the criterion over time, the ratio of positive to negative points should remain at 3 to 1.

If you are concerned that your students may not be successful in the Good Behavior Game, try this variation. Instead of listing "-1 Point" inappropriate behaviors, simply list the "+3 Points" appropriate behaviors. Tally three points on the blackboard if the entire class is engaging in one of the listed behaviors when the tape beeps. If a student is not engaging in one of the listed behaviors when the tape beeps, do not write any marks on the blackboard. Don't subtract any either.

There are several considerations that arise with group-oriented contingencies. The major concern is not the use of peer pressure, which already exists in the classroom, but the systematic use of peer pressure to modify the behavior of students. This concern can be addressed by reducing the chances of scapegoating. **Scapegoating** occurs when peers target one student to be the object of ridicule or blame when points are not earned. When implementing a group-oriented contingency in your classroom, you may want to incorporate some of the strategies for reducing scapegoating found in *Table 3-2*.

One of the biggest threats to the success of a group-oriented contingency is sabotage. **Sabotage** occurs when a student purposely undermines a group's best efforts. Some students may find it more reinforcing to sabotage the group-oriented contingency than to receive the reinforcer. Remember, all behaviors are purposeful—they are performed to accomplish a specific outcome. In sabotaging the contingency, students are often being reinforced by acquiring power and control. If sabotage occurs, it is helpful to conduct a functional assessment to determine why the student is sabotaging. If a student who is sabotaging is trying to acquire power and control, you can try to find a more powerful reinforcer than the power and control—a truly daunting task. Or, you can eliminate the student from the group-oriented contingency by having him or her watch, but not participate. If you eliminate the student from the contingency, then it is important to place him or her on an individual behavior management intervention (such as Chart Move, Mystery Motivator, Spinner, or 49 Square Chart). Otherwise, the student will engage in disruptive behavior to obtain attention or power and control while the rest of the class participates in the group-oriented contingency.

Chapter 10

Conducting Functional Assessments

Conducting functional assessment is the second interrelated component of managing resistance. The first component, analyzing and manipulating context, was described previously. The third component—being comprehensive and unrestricting in our behavior—will be discussed in Part IV. Used together, these three interrelated components are highly effective in managing resistance.

By now you probably have a good understanding that all behavior is purposeful and that analyzing and manipulating context while ignoring the function of a behavior will not be very effective. Recall the context manipulation study conducted by Ayllon (1963) described in Chapter 2. In this study the context surrounding a behavior (towel hoarding) was changed. In addition to changing the context, a replacement behavior must be provided—a behavior that allows the student to accomplish the same goal as the inappropriate behavior. If a replacement behavior is not provided, the student will simply perform other inappropriate behaviors that serve the same function that the original inappropriate behavior served.

Functional assessment is a way of determining the function (i.e., purpose, intent, outcome, and goal) of a given behavior. Once we determine the function, we can effectively manipulate the envi-

ronment and teach replacement behaviors in order to reduce resistance and increase adaptive behavioral repertoire (the number of appropriate behaviors displayed). The two basic concerns of functional assessment, the contextual nature of behavior and the purposefulness of behavior, dovetail with the strategies presented in this book. Conducting functional assessments is a natural—and necessary—component of managing resistance.

Simply stated, functional assessment accomplishes two purposes:

1. Identifying environmental factors that affect the performance of a behavior and the desired outcome that the behavior serves.

2. Identifying a replacement behavior that is an appropriate way for the student to obtain the desired goal.

Factors affecting the performance of inappropriate behavior are identified, appropriate replacement behaviors are selected, and appropriate interventions are implemented based on three types of hypotheses: functional, contextual, and curricular.

Functional hypotheses are testable guesses that are related to the function, or the intent, of a behavior. Neel and Cessna (1993) developed a classification system of behavioral intent (see *Table 3-3*) to determine the reason a student engages in a specific behavior. A functional hypothesis that "Jane tantrums in order to get the teacher's attention" focuses on the desired outcome or purpose of Jane's behavior. Functional hypotheses address replacement behavior training—teaching an appropriate behavior that serves the same purpose as an inappropriate behavior. A replacement behavior is likely to result in a gener-alized and durable decrease in the target behavior if it is found to be an acceptable alternative for the student. Once we determine the intent (i.e., purpose, function, outcome, goal, reason) a behavior serves, we can teach and reinforce a student for performing a **replacement behavior**—an appropriate behavior that serves the same purpose as the inappropriate behavior. Then the student will "give up" misbehaving because he or she can get what is wanted appropriately.

Contextual hypotheses focus on analyzing the antecedents and consequences surrounding a behavior. One of the most basic and best ways to generate contextual hypotheses is through the use of an A-B-C analysis (see *Figures 3-1 and Table 3-1*). Contextual hypotheses result in modifying some aspect of the environment, for example, moving the student who makes animal noises to the other

Classification of Behavioral Intent	
Strategy	**Description**
Power/Control	When a child's outcome is the control of events and/or situations; Characterized by a child acting to stay in a situation and keep control.
Protection/Escape Avoidance	When a child's outcome is to avoid a task or activity; escape a consequence; or termi-nate or leave a situation.
Attention	When a child becomes the focus of a situation; draws attention to self; result is that the child puts himself/herself in the foreground of a situation; discriminates self from group for a period of time; distinguishing feature is "becoming the focus" as the end product of the behavior.
Acceptance/Affiliation	When a child connects/relates with others; mutuality of benefit is present.
Expression of Self	When a child develops a forum of expression; could be statements of needs or percep-tions, or demonstration of skills and talents.
Gratification	When a child is self-rewarded or pleased; distinguishing characteristic is that reward is self-determined; others may play agent role.
Justice/Revenge	When a child settles a difference; provides restitution, or demonstrates contrition; set-tling the score.

Table 3-3

Note. From "Behavioral Intent: Instructional content for students with behavior disorders" by Neel, R.S. and Cessna, K.K. (1993). In Cessna, K.K. (Ed.), *Instructionally differentiated programming: A needs-based approach for students with behavior disorders* (p.35), Denver, CO: Colorado Department of Education. Copyright © 1993 by Cessna, K.K., Jefferson County Schools, Golden, CO. Reprinted with permission.

side of the classroom, away from the peers who reinforce her behavior.

Curricular hypotheses focus on identifying the curricular demands that accompany the inappropriate behavior and then modifying the presentation of the curriculum to encourage appropriate behavior. Curricular variables (e.g., student preference, choice-making, length of task, type of task, and task difficulty) influence noncompliant behavior. Often noncompliant behavior functions as a means to escape difficult academic activities.

Hypothesis Development

The first stage of functional assessment is generating hypotheses (our best guesses) as to the function of a noncompliant behavior. To generate these hypotheses we collect information from a variety of sources and instruments. We conduct interviews and review archival data (e.g., psychological reports, standardized testing, student assistance team reports, and individualized education programs). We complete rating scales and directly observe students.

This process proceeds from global behavioral information to more specific information. For example, we observe that a student continually interrupts peer conversations or games during recess (one of the diagnostic criteria for ADHD). We hypothesize that the student interrupts conversations because that is the only way he knows how to obtain attention from peers. Although his peers respond to the intrusion negatively, negative attention still acts as a reinforcer. From this first general hypothesis, we generate and test more specific hypotheses. For example, we reinforce the peers when they ignore the student's inappropriate behavior and reinforce the student when he engages in appropriate behavior. If

appropriate behavior results from these contextual manipulations, then we have determined the functional relation between the behavior, the outcome desired by the student, and the impact of the peers' responses on the behavior.

To develop hypotheses, begin with these four steps:

1. Precisely define the behavior of concern (the target behavior).

2. Interview adults (and students when appropriate) to determine environmental factors that affect the behavior.

3. Directly observe the target behavior in the natural setting.

4. Develop the hypotheses.

1. Precisely define the behavior of concern (the target behavior).

It is necessary to precisely define a behavior, so that its occurrences and nonoccurrences can be reliably noted. Defining a behavior as "strikes other students on the back with open hand for two seconds, five times a day" is preferable to "hits other students a lot." Those who work most closely with a student can often offer the most specific behavioral definition. Precisely defining the behavior ensures that everyone involved in the functional assessment is observing the same thing.

A behavior is operationally defined when it passes the Stranger Test (Kaplan, 1995). This means that someone not familiar with the student could read the definition of the target behavior and accurately determine its occurrence or nonoccurrence at a level comparable to that of staff members. If a stranger observed the frequency of a student's "hostility," would the stranger's count of the occurrences differ substantially from the teacher's count? The stranger might interpret "hostility" as "hits," "bites," "shoves," and "kicks," whereas the teacher might define "hostility" as "uses provocative language" (i.e., verbal threats or profanity directed at peers). However, if the teacher has defined "hostility" as "each instance of an unprovoked hit," and further defined "unprovoked" as "not in retaliation for a physical or verbal attack," both the stranger and the teacher would likely arrive at the same count of occurrences.

2. **Interview to determine environmental factors that affect the behavior.**

   Interviewing adults (and students when appropriate) is essential when gathering information about antecedents and consequences surrounding behavior. Dunlap and Kern (1993) recommended interviewing at least two school personnel who are involved with the student and the student's parents. The purpose of interviewing multiple people is to determine if certain behaviors occur in some, but not other, contexts. Dunlap and Kern (1993) also recommended asking the following questions during an interview:

   1. How long have you known the student?

   2. How much time do you spend with the student per week?

   3. What do you see as the major problems from most to least severe?

   4. In what situations do these behaviors occur?

   5. In what situations are the behaviors most appropriate?

   6. What are the student's best strengths?

   7. What are the student's worst weaknesses?

   8. Why do you think the student behaves the way he or she does?

   9. What do you think should be done to help the student?

   10. What does the student like most?

   11. What does the student like least?

   12. What events or actions seem to trigger noncompliant behavior?

   13. What do you think can be done to increase the student being compliant?

The information collected through interviewing is fairly general and often appears in nonbehavioral terms. For example, one teacher may say a student is off-task during most independent seatwork while another teacher may say that the student is inattentive during lectures. "Off-task" and "inattentive" are not specific behaviors. Nevertheless, this information provides a contextual starting point to formulate a hypothesis. The hypothesis can then be tested using methods of direct observation.

3. **Directly observe the target behavior in the natural setting.**

   Direct observation is necessary for determining environmental factors that maintain noncompliant behavior or prevent the performance of compliant behavior. Direct observation of student's behavior helps us to:

   1. Confirm (or deny) a relation between behavior and environmental events.

   2. Formulate solid pre-intervention information and use that information to determine the extent of noncompliant behavior

Student: Mary Smith   **Dates:** 4/1 to 4/12

Behavior: refuses to follow directions   **Observer:** Mr. Wilson

Activity	Time	Days									
		M	T	W	TH	F	M	T	W	TH	F
Warm Up	8:30-9:00	O		O	X		O				
Reading Groups	9:00-9:30	O					X				
Spelling	9:30-10:00	X					O				
Recess/Story	10:00-10:30										
Math	10:30-11:00	X	O		X	X	X		O		O
Lunch	11:00-11:30										
Free Read	11:30-12:00	X					O				
Social Studies	12:00-12:30						X				
Art/Music/Health	12:30-1:00									O	
Phys. Ed.	1:00-1:30		O								
Science	1:30-2:00				O						
Catch Up	2:00-2:30	X					O				
Prepare for Home	2:30-3:00										

Figure 3-14

An example of a scatter plot for observing behavior.

Note. From Using Functional Assessment to Develop Effective, Individualized Interventions for Challenging Behaviors by L. Foster-Johnson and G. Dunlap, 1993, *Teaching Exceptional Children*, 25 (3), p. 48 © 1993by Council for Exceptional Children. Reprinted with permission.

and the effects of environmental and replacement behavior manipulations.

One of the most effective, systematic approaches for directly observing behavior is the **scatter plot** (Foster-Johnson & Dunlap, 1993) depicted in *Figure 3-14*.

The scatter plot divides two weeks of school into units (class periods and days of the week). Using the scatter plot, we can observe and chart occurrences and nonoccurrences of a behavior over a period of two weeks, making it possible for us to identify patterns. The scatter plot in *Figure 3-14* reveals that the math period seems to be a particularly important antecedent for the occurrence of noncompliance. From this information, it is helpful to do a more specific A-B-C analysis during math time to determine specific math antecedents related to the noncompliant behavior. Conversely, recess/story time and preparing for home have no

episodes of noncompliant behavior. These activities may be used as a powerful reinforcer to maintain compliant behavior at other times. In addition, this scatter plot indicates that more noncompliant behavior occurs on Mondays than on any other day of the week. A blank scatter plot is included as part of the "Functional Assessment Hypotheses Formulation Protocol" in the Reproducibles section.

Remember that a hypothesis simply represents your best guess. Don't be discouraged if your first hypothesis does not work out. The very nature of functional assessment is to disprove hypotheses as much as it is to prove them. Disproving a hypothesis provides information useful in developing the next hypothesis to test.

4. Develop the hypotheses.

Although you can generate hypotheses and effective interventions, the process can be time

consuming. Many interview and direct observation approaches also require extensive assistance by a consultant or specialist well-versed in functional assessment. To help teachers conduct functional assessments independently, Larson and Maag (1998) developed a simple protocol. This protocol, provided in the Reproducibles section, addresses all of the steps in the hypotheses development stage of functional assessment. It will help you to arrive at a plan for contextual, curricular, and replacement strategies.

The protocol directs the observer through the process of operationally defining the target behavior, identifying setting events (antecedents) and functions (intents) associated with the target behavior, and conducting a systematic observation. The culmination is hypothesis statement and a functional analysis plan.

Hypothesis Testing

The second stage of functional assessment, often referred to as functional analysis, consists of testing hypotheses by manipulating events and behaviors related to functions believed to prompt

and maintain the target behavior. For example, a student refuses to follow directions. If the hypothesized function of the student's refusal is to escape from a difficult task, then the functional analysis plan might be to remove task demands, while holding other behavioral and environmental variables constant. If the target behavior decreases, then task demands can be reintroduced to further test the hypothesis. If the target behavior then increases, task demands are most likely a relevant and controlling variable.

Hypotheses related to the function of the target behavior can also be tested. For example, the student can be taught and reinforced for using the replacement behavior of "requesting a break from the task." If the target behavior further decreases, then the functional hypothesis was corroborated. There are four steps to testing a hypothesis:

1. Specifically define the target behavior.

2. Select a recording method for observing and counting the occurrences of the target behavior (see *Table 3-4*).

3. Observe the target behavior before and after manipulating curricular, contextual, or functional variables.

4. Graph the results of the behavioral observations as a visual representation of the effects of the manipulations.

Choosing a Recording Method

An overview of the four recording methods is provided in *Table 3-4*. It's important to choose the method that best fits the situation, so that you have a clear indication of how behavior changes when you manipulate variables.

Frequency recording involves tallying the number of times a targeted behavior occurs. It is the most

An Overview of Functional Assessment Recording Methods		
Recording Method	**Description**	**Indications**
Frequency Recording	Count the number of times a target behavior occurs.	Appropriate for behaviors with short movement cycle; inappropriate for high rate behaviors or those occurring over an extended period of time.
Duration Recording	Measure how long a behavior lasts.	Appropriate for behaviors that occur infrequently but continue for long periods of time.
Interval Recording	Measure occurrence or nonoccurrence of behavior within specified intervals. A mark is made if behavior occurred during any part of interval (partial) or entire interval (whole); percentage of intervals marked is computed.	Provides estimate of both frequency and duration; easy to use this technique; disadvantage is that it requires observer's undivided attention.
Time Sampling	Same as interval recording except observer looks at student at end of interval and records if behavior is or is not occurring at that instant.	Does not require observer's undivided attention; allows for longer interval lengths than interval recording.

Table 3-4
Choose a recording method for observing the occurrences of the target behavior.

commonly used technique and the most advantageous in that it is fairly easy to do and produces a number (of total occurrences) that can be graphed. It can be applied to many disruptive behaviors in the classroom, such as "hits the peers," "runs out of the room," "raises hand," and "asks for help." The number of times a student engages in a target behavior can be tallied on such easy-to-carry devices as wrist counters; hand-tally digital counters; wrist tally boards; masking tape wrapped around your wrist; or pennies, buttons, or paper clips that can be moved from one pocket to another each time the target behavior occurs. Additionally, a Frequency Recording Sheet is provided in the Reproducibles section.

Duration recording is used when we need to measure how long a behavior lasts. It its most appropriate for behaviors that occur infrequently but continue for some length of time or for behaviors that occur at such a high rate that one

episode blends into the next. Duration recording might be appropriate for these behaviors.

- Crying
- Writing a paper
- Drumming on the desk top
- Minutes it takes to get back to the class after the recess bell
- Time it takes to finish a math assignment

Because these behaviors are more aptly described by how long they last rather than simply the number of times they occur, it is better to use duration recording than frequency recording. It is more important to know that "Li cried for 12 minutes without stopping" than simply "Li cried one time today;" or that "Paula was out of her seat for 17 minutes, then 10 minutes, then 23 minutes," rather than simply "Paula was out of her seat three times today." You can record duration by noting it on a piece of paper (or on the Duration Recording Sheet provided in the Reproducibles section).

Interval recording measures the occurrence or nonoccurrence of a behavior within specified time intervals. The total observation time is divided into equal intervals, and the observer records whether or not the behavior occurs during those intervals. The length of the intervals usually ranges from 5 to 30 seconds. A blank Interval Recording Sheet is provided in the Reproducibles section. *Figure 3-15* shows how the sheet should be filled out for a 5-minute interval. Each row represents the passage of 1 minute.

To construct your interval recording sheet, first determine how long the observation period is to last then divide it into 5-second intervals. For a 5-minute observation, you would divide the period into 10-second intervals:

1. Convert the total observation period into seconds (5 minutes x 60 seconds=300).

2. Choose interval length (10 seconds).

3. Divide total observation period into 10 second intervals (300 ÷ 10=30).

4. Set up a recording sheet with the total number of observation intervals for this period (30).

To use the observation, we make only one mark in each box depending on whether or not the target behavior occurred. If the target behavior occurred during any part of a 10-second interval, then a "X" is placed in that box. If the target behavior did not occur at all during the 10-second interval, then an "O" is placed in that box. Only one mark is made per interval. It does not matter whether the target behavior occurred once or five times during a given 10-second interval. We still only mark one "X" in the interval box. If a student talks to her neighbor three times during a 10-second interval–once each at the beginning, middle, and end of the interval–only one mark is made for the occurrence of the behavior during that interval.

Because we are dividing an observation into intervals, the results are shown in terms of percentage. We do not record the total number of "X"s appearing on the observation form. Remember one "X" could represent any number of times the behavior occurred during a given 10-second interval. Instead, we are interested in the **percentage of intervals** in which the child engaged in the target behavior. In the example there are a total of 30 intervals. If the student engaged in the target behavior during 12 of those intervals, then the student engaged in the target behavior during 40% of the observation period.

Time sampling is a type of interval recording. In this approach, the tar-

---

5-Minute Interval Recording Sheet

Student: _____

Date: _____

Observer _____ Time Began: _____

Time Ended: _____

Target Behavior: _____

Directions: Place an "X" in the interval boxes in which the target behavior occurred and a "O" in the interval boxes in which the target behavior did not occur.

Total Observation Time Equals 5 Minutes

	10 Seconds	10 Seconds	10 Seconds	10 Seconds	10 Seconds
1 Minute					
2 Minutes					
3 Minutes					
4 Minutes					
5 Minutes					

Figure 3-15
An Interval Recording Sheet set up for 5-minute intervals.

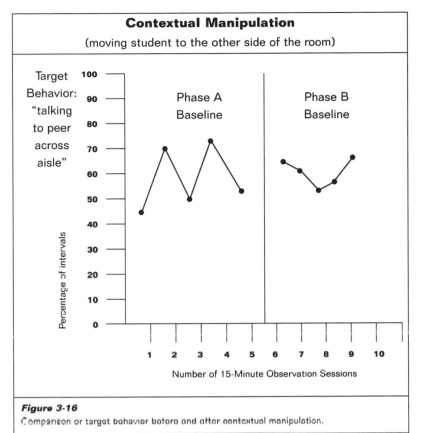

Figure 3-16

Comparison or target behavior before and after contextual manipulation.

Graphing Your Observations

To graph the results of observing and recording a target behavior, you'll need to set up a graph with horizontal and vertical axes on which to mark the number of observation sessions and target behavior, respectively. (See Figure *3-16* and the blank graph in the Reproducibles section.) Before you begin your intervention, you will need to graph the **baseline** (the occurrences of the target behavior prior to intervention). In *Figure 3-16*, each data point represents the number of times the target behavior occurred during one observation session. Once you record a data point for each observation session, connect the points

get behavior is recorded only if it occurs at the end of the interval. Unlike interval recording in which we are concerned with whether or not the behavior occurred at all during the interval, the time sampling procedure only requires us to be interested in whether the behavior occurred immediately following an interval. The process of creating a time sampling recording sheet is the same as that employed with interval recording. You can also use the Interval Recording Sheet in the Reproducibles section when doing time sampling.

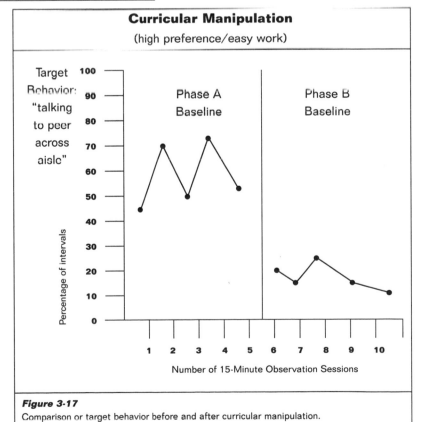

Figure 3-17

Comparison or target behavior before and after curricular manipulation.

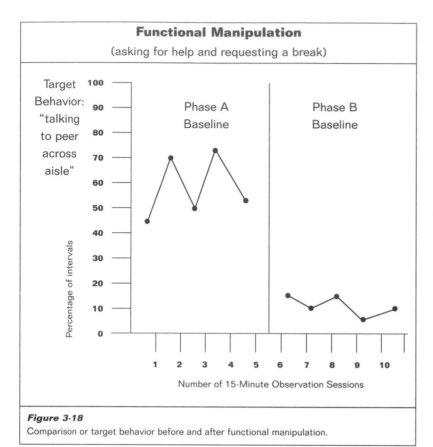

Functional Manipulation

(asking for help and requesting a break)

Target Behavior: "talking to peer across aisle"

Percentage of intervals

Phase A Baseline

Phase B Baseline

Number of 15-Minute Observation Sessions

Figure 3-18

Comparison or target behavior before and after functional manipulation.

phase change (when baseline ended and the manipulation began). In functional analysis (the hypothesis-testing stage of functional assessment), the "B" phase designates the onset of a manipulation, whether it is contextual, curricular, or functional.

Figure 3-16 depicts the percentage of intervals during which the student talked to his peer before and after the contextual manipulation of moving him to the opposite side of the room. In both phases, the occurrence of the target behavior remained relatively stable. Therefore, it does not seem that the student's goal is to affiliate with any particular peer but rather to talk to anyone sitting across the aisle.

This will provide a visual representation that allows you to easily determine whether a behavior is increasing or decreasing during the baseline.

Once you have graphed the baseline, you can do the same for the behavioral observations you make after manipulating contextual, curricular, or functional variables. You'll need to graph each variable separately. *Figures 3-16*, *3-17*, and *3-18* compare the baseline of a target behavior to the number of occurrences after manipulations.

The target behavior graphed in each of the three figures is "talks to peer across aisle." A 15-minute time sampling technique (see *Table 3-4*) was chosen to record this behavior. Therefore, the data are plotted as a percentage of intervals. Phase A in each of the three figures refers to the baseline. The vertical line dividing the graph indicates a

Given the results depicted in *Figure 3-15*, a different type of manipulation is warranted. *Figure 3-17* presents the results of a curricular hypothesis that talking is a way to escape a task the student finds difficult. To test this hypothesis, the student was given high preference, relatively easy work to complete during Phase B instead of the more difficult work typically assigned. As a result of this curricular manipulation, the occurrence of the target behavior decreased substantially. Therefore, the curricular hypothesis that the student talked to avoid difficult work is confirmed.

Based on these results, a third hypothesis is generated using a functional manipulation. The student is taught two replacement behaviors: asking for help when the assignment becomes too difficult and asking for a break when becoming frustrated. *Figure 3-18* shows that these replacement behaviors resulted in a further decrease in the target behavior. Remember, replacement behaviors often result in a generalized and durable decrease in the target behavior when a student finds them acceptable. Therefore, the student can use the behaviors across a wide variety of settings and tasks.

Testing hypotheses helps us determine the most effective approach for managing resistance. Let's revisit the use of the "do-nothing chair" to examine this point. Recall that the "do-nothing chair" is effective when passivity serves the function of power and control. Recall also that the "do-nothing chair" will not work when the function of passivity is escape/avoidance from a task for which the student does not possess the requisite skills, when he or she finds the task boring or irrelevant.

We can use functional assessment to determine whether passivity serves the function of power/control or escape/avoidance. The best place to start is testing the hypothesis that passivity is a way for a student to escape or avoid a difficult or boring task. We can test this hypothesis by giving the student a high interest task. Let us assume that the task is completing a math worksheet. Let us also assume that the student loves to draw more than any other activity. Instead of giving the student a math assignment, we provide a new pad of drawing paper and pens. We then direct the student to draw whatever she wants. We phrase the drawing assignment as a demand in order to bring out any power/control that may be fueling passivity. If the student begins to draw, our hypothesis that passivity serves an escape/avoidance function is confirmed. In this case, there was no need for the student to be passive when given something to do that she liked.

If the student refuses to follow the direction to draw (engage in a high preference activity), then we know that passivity serves the function of

power/control. In other words, the reinforcing value of engaging in a high preference activity was not as great as the reinforcing value of obtaining power and control. In this case, functional assessment has revealed that the "do-nothing chair" will be an effective intervention. If, however, the student's passivity serves the function of escape/avoidance, then we still need to design an intervention. Here is one approach. We can tell the student that we understand that she does not like completing the math assignments, but that there are better ways to communicate this message than sitting passively. We also give her a two-minute break every time she can verbally request one. Furthermore, every time she asks to take a break (instead of sitting passively), we give her one extra minute to shoot baskets in the gym (assuming she finds this activity reinforcing). In this way, we doubly reinforce the student's replacement behavior.

You may think that students will manipulate this contingency by continually asking to take a break. The hope is that this will actually happen! The student has been using passivity to escape from a task. Through repetition, passivity has become habitual and used automatically. When the student continually asks to take a break, she is practicing a new behavior. By asking for breaks, she is not being passive. Because our previous efforts at managing the student's resistance have failed, we also have nothing to lose. No work was being completed anyway. After a couple of weeks, if the student is still continuously requesting breaks, we tell the student that we are pleased that she has become so good at asking for breaks, but that we are not sure if she needs to ask for breaks as often. We also say that we will give the student 2 minutes of free time for every 10 minutes that pass in which she refrains from taking a break. Now the student is being doubly reinforced for going longer periods without breaks. At the same time, we want the math assignment itself to be so manageable (maybe no more than one or two problems to begin with) that the student will not be overwhelmed.

PART IV

Changing Our Behavior

A man who had been hiking in the desert enters a tavern, walks up to the bartender, slams his fist on the bar and says, "Water!" The bartender briefly turns away and bends down to retrieve something. When he again faces the man, he has a pistol behind his back that he quickly brings about face and fires once straight up in the air. The man pauses for a second, smiles, says "Thank you," and walks out of the tavern.

Chapter 11

Overcoming Limitations

I often begin my workshops on managing resistance with this story. I then ask the participants to figure out why the man, who requested water but received none, would say "thank you" and leave the tavern satisfied. In order to help with this task, participants can ask me any question that can be answered with a "yes" or "no." Here is a sampling of the most frequently asked questions:

"Was there water in a tank above the man?"

"Was the gun loaded?"

"Was the gun a water pistol?"

"Did the man want a bath?"

"Did the man know the bartender?"

"Did both men speak the same language?"

None of these questions are relevant to solving the riddle. Instead, the most relevant question is "Was the man thirsty?" The answer is no. The answer to the riddle is that the man had hiccups.

This riddle is a potent paradigm story. Recall that in Part I paradigm was defined as a pattern or model for interpreting information. It establishes boundaries and provides a framework for perceived information by solving problems within those given boundaries (Barker, 1992). We all view the world through paradigms—constantly selecting from the environment those data that best fit our view of the world, while trying to ignore the rest. As a result, what is perfectly obvious to a person adhering to one paradigm may be totally imperceptible to a person with a different paradigm.

In the preceding riddle, most people assume that asking for water means the man was either thirsty or dirty. Of course, the statement that the man had been walking in the desert is misleading. Most people are constrained by their paradigms and cannot access other options in their repertoire (i.e., that drinking water and being startled are remedies for hiccups). In Part I this condition was referred to as paradigm paralysis.

The cure for paradigm paralysis is to be comprehensive and unrestricting in our thought processes. This gives us access to knowledge and skills that are otherwise not perceived as options.

It is amazing what we could do if we perceived all our available options. It is estimated that we average one billion experiences in any twenty-year period. Individuals are aware of approximately 40 percent of their total experiences. Out of that 40 percent, individuals may recall only 1 percent. The point I am making in terms of managing resistance is that we have much more knowledge than we allow into our process. The two main goals of Part IV are:

1. To remember what we have forgotten.

2. To understand the difference between knowledge and knowing.

These two goals are interrelated. In order to understand the difference between knowledge and knowing, we must remember what we have forgotten. For example, most of us possess the knowledge that hiccups can be cured by drinking water and being startled. Yet, we forgot that information because we were constrained by our paradigms. In other words, we had the knowledge to solve the riddle, but we did not know that we knew. This is the difference between knowledge and knowing. Knowing is much more important than knowledge. We accumulate a vast knowledge base over the course of many years. The challenge is to access that knowledge by being comprehensive and unrestricting. Unfettered by convention, we can overcome our limitations.

Overcoming limitations is difficult not only because we are constrained by our paradigms, but also because we experience stress when we work with students with challenging behaviors. When we experience stress, we tend to revert to habitual and automatic behaviors. For example, let's say you implement the "do-nothing chair" strategy with a student. After exuding a nonchalant and encouraging attitude about being pleased that the student can get really good at doing nothing, he looks you in the face and calls you a jerk. Most of us would be offended by being called a jerk and

"We have much more knowledge than we let ourselves know."

"Be personal, but don't personalize students' behavior."

take this insult personally. We would then revert to a punitive mentality, which would only reinforce the student's opposition. Chapter 11 describes an approach for maintaining our emotional and behavioral control—keeping our cool in the face of insults and goading. It is much easier for us to access our knowledge when we can maintain our cool.

Chapter 3 provides four additional techniques for managing resistance: paradoxical directives, therapeutic metaphors, reframing, and surprise and shock. These four techniques require analyzing and manipulating context. They also require us to be comprehensive and unrestricting.

If we perceive all our available options we can be much more effective at managing resistance. Unfortunately, we typically follow a routine, not realizing that we are restricting our behavior. We limit our options to certain ways of behaving, based on how we handled a situation previously. This phenomenon results in the applications of linear interventions (Watzlawick, Weakland, & Fisch, 1974). Linear interventions are simply "more of the same" and seldom work. An example of a linear intervention is keeping a student after school for misbehaving. When the student misbehaves the following day, we keep him or her after school again—even though this intervention did not work the first time.

Recall the example of punishment in the "Consequent Manipulations" section of Part III. If punishment was effective, it would be used *less*, not more, because by definition *punishment* decreases behavior (Maag, 1999). Our

blind adherence to the punishment paradigm illustrates how easily we fall into the trap of doing the same thing over and over, even when it is not working. There is truth in the axiom, "If what we are doing is not working, try something else—anything else!" Once I was asked if it was important to be consistent with students. My reply was "If being consistent is working." Certainly it is important to be consistent—a point advocated in Maag (1996). But, it is more important to not blindly adhere to one way of doing things to the exclusion of other options.

Milton Erickson did not allow himself to be fettered by convention. Rossi, Ryan, and Sharp (1983) described how Erickson was asked to take part in a consultation regarding a patient who was catatonic schizophrenic and not responding to treatment. Erickson walked into the room where the patient was sitting in a catatonic state. Several psychiatrists were discussing various conventional psychiatric interventions that could be used, including psychotropic medication and electroconvulsive shock therapy. Without hesitation, Erickson walked over to the patient and stomped on his feet several times. The patient immediately snapped out of the catatonic state. The point is not that foot stomping would result in long-term change, but that many potential interventions are available if we shed our paradigms and access other areas of our experience.

Here's another example of overcoming limitations. During my workshops, I often instruct every other person in the audience to make a fist. People are then asked to try to open the fist of the person sitting to their left as quickly as possible. Inevitably, most people try to force the person's fist open. The following question is then presented to the group: "How many people simply *asked* the person to open his or her fist?" Very few people will have tried this technique; although all will readily acknowledge possessing the skill in their repertoires. Sometimes I simply ask those who still have their fists clenched to raise their hands. Then I walk over and extend my hand to congratulate a person on being so persistent. Most often, the person shakes my hand, thereby releasing their fist.

There are four goals we must achieve in order to overcome limitations:

1. Do not take your students' behaviors personally.

2. Do not be afraid to respond differently.

3. Do not exercise cold, hard judgment.

4. Do not limit your patterns of responding.

All of these goals focus on changing *our* behavior—not the behavior of our students. We cannot compel students to behave in certain ways. We can *influence* them, but we cannot force them to comply. On the other hand, we have complete control over our own behavior. And we have the ability to modify our behavior continuously until we receive the desired response. This task is made easier when we recognize and understand the four goals that enable us to respond creatively.

1. **Do not take your students' behaviors personally.**

Most of us take personally the behaviors of our students. This is also true of parents, especially parents of teenagers who exert their independence by being defiant and disrespect-

ful. In this situation, we may feel hurt that our children are not treating us as well as they did in earlier in years. We may react with anger (the common way to demonstrate that we feel hurt) and try to force them to comply (a misdirected effort to feel better about ourselves). This also happens in the classroom. We may spend considerable time planning lessons only to have some students express that the lesson is "boring" and "stupid." We take these "insults" personally. Again, we feel hurt, and often display anger. Showing anger makes us appear less emotionally vulnerable than showing hurt. Getting angry may also result in students feeling hurt, thereby giving them a "dose of their own medicine." But once we display anger, the students have the upper hand—we have given them power and control. Chapter 13 provides approaches that will to help us not take behaviors personally.

2. **Do not be afraid to respond differently.**

We often find it risky to respond in a way that is different from our normal course of action. We strive for consistency. Consistency breeds predictability, which engenders feelings of comfort. When we try something new we lose predictability. Recall the example in Chapter 2 of Freud's theory of resistance. He speculated that resistance maintains our internal equilibrium and helps us avoid anxiety associated with changing our behavior. Recall also how, from a family systems viewpoint, we prefer to cling to the way things *are* rather than expose ourselves to the uncertainty and threat implied by changing our behavior. Consequently, we tend to react to students in consistent ways, even if we are not obtaining the results we desire. This predictability leads to the application of linear interventions. Unfortunately, doing "more of the same" makes difficulties more severe because the initial problem was mishandled and remains unresolved.

Shedding our conventional patterns of responding can dramatically improve our ability to manage resistance. We want to access all our experiences to provide students with an unconventional response. The unexpected always helps us deal with resistance. It creates confusion for the student. It is difficult for students to be resistant when they are confused because they don't know how we'll respond. This breaks the stimulus-response chain of resistant behavior.

3. Do not exercise cold, hard judgment.

We tend to exercise cold, hard judgment when dealing with challenging behaviors. Judgment is based on our value system and is developed from past experiences with family, community, religion, media, and other parts of society. The standards we impose come from our values. If a student's behavior is not aligned with our standards, then we judge that a problem exists. However, our judgment may be biased by such factors as a student's gender, ethnicity, physical appearance, and our perception of the cause of the behavior. Furthermore, we are more likely to uphold special standards for a specific student if we perceive the cause of their misbehavior to be internal (e.g., a medical problem). Many educators apply higher standards for students with challenging behaviors. If we expect a student to behave exceptionally well, then we believe it will be easier to manage his or her behavior. It is as if we obtain a sense of security from this notion. The result, of course, is that we set up the student to misbehave.

4. Do not limit your patterns of responding.

Initial attempts at managing challenging behaviors are frequently based on formal training. We view management techniques obtained from college courses, professors, and textbooks as originating from "experts." We often consider this information as "gospel" and, consequently, limit our ways of dealing with resistance to these approaches. There is nothing inherently wrong in the techniques the "experts" espouse. However, managing resistance requires that we not adhere to any "cookbook" approach. There is no "magic bullet" for managing resistance.

What if we accessed all of the experiences of our life? We can access our experiences of dealing with Uncle Harry's pontifications at Thanksgiving dinner or a rude cashier at a department store to manage resistance. So often we think we are watching everything, but we are not really watching because we have a routine way of looking.

Children have open minds—they see much more than do we. They are also much more creative. That creativity is unfortunately conditioned out of us by the time we graduate from high school. But if we go into any kindergarten classroom, draw a dot on the blackboard, and ask what it is, we receive hundreds of creative answers: "a black hole," "a caterpillar egg," "a bug," "a secret passageway," "a tunnel," and many more. If we can go into a high school classroom and draw the same dot on the blackboard, we usually get only two answers to our question: "dot" and "period." As we get older, our creativity is expunged. However, we are generally a resilient and creative species that can overcome the limitations we've acquired through the years. We can tap our resourcefulness to manage resistance more effectively.

Chapter 12

Strategies for Controlling Our Emotions and Behavior

Most of this book focuses on the role of context and the function of behavior. Embedded in these discussions and intervention techniques is the notion that we need to be flexible and access experiences that we do not normally bring into play when managing challenging behaviors. The very nature of using the expression "a student with challenging behaviors" indicates that our traditional approaches have failed. If our current approaches worked, a student's behavior would not be a challenge!

Most of our attempts to limit our overreacting and counterproductive behaviors have limited or short term success. What we really need is a system for permanently changing our emotional reactions and behavioral responses. Once we learn this system, we can stubbornly refuse to make ourselves miserable about how others behave, no matter how disagreeable.

The following approach will help you to not become emotionally upset, thereby enabling you to access a more desirable response. This approach is based on Ellis' Rational-Emotive Therapy, or RET (Ellis, 1962). RET teaches us how to react more productively by applying logical, rational thinking. RET is a re-educative model that emphasizes accountability and evaluation. Its approach for promoting change is structured

and systematic. More than a series of techniques, RET is a unique philosophy of life. It can help us avoid overreacting emotionally when confronted with disagreeable situations. The goal of RET is to help us identify our irrational beliefs, challenge them, and correct our mistakes in reasoning. By doing this, we can sustain the emotional strength to deal with others effectively.

Four Parts to Experience

The initial step of RET is understanding the four components of experience: event, belief, emotion, and behavior. **Event** refers to any situation of which we are a part. It includes our interactions with others. **Belief** refers to interpretation, or the meaning we attach to the event or situation.

Emotion refers to the feelings we experience: happiness, sadness, anger, frustration, anxiety, depression, guilt, joy, and so forth. **Behavior** refers to our actions—how we respond both verbally and nonverbally when confronted with a situation.

Many of us incorrectly think the situations and people we encounter lead us to specific feelings. We often say things like, "That student makes me so angry when he talks back to me" or "Speaking in front of others makes me nervous." What we fail to understand is that the way others treat us has nothing to do with how we feel and behave. How we make ourselves feel and behave is based on our beliefs. We always have choices as to what we believe. The critical component is the belief we hold.

Because we erroneously believe others are responsible for our negative feelings, we try to make them stop whatever it is they are doing. Usually we fail miserably at this task. But how can the same event result in experiencing two radically different emotions? The answer is that the event doesn't create the emotion. Our beliefs do. Often we assign meaning by relating an event to past experience. The following story of Wally and Marge illustrates this point:

> Wally and Marge have been dating for several months. The courtship is progressing nicely as both of them move toward a more intimate and meaningful relationship. Wally's line of work requires him to be out of town several days month. Upon returning from a business trip, he typically goes to see Marge at her apartment. On this visit, when Marge answers the door, Wally presents her with a dozen long-stemmed roses. Marge looks at the roses and then at Wally. A big smile crosses her face as she joyfully gives Wally a big hug and kiss, saying how much she loves him.

This interaction can be broken down into the four components:

1. **Event:** Wally gives Marge roses.

2. **Belief:** Marge tells herself Wally cares about her.

3. **Emotion:** Marge feels happy.

4. **Behavior:** Marge tells Wally she loves him and gives him a hug and kiss.

In the following version of the story, the outcome changes even though the event is the same.

> Wally and Marge have been dating for several months. The courtship is progressing nicely as both of them move toward a more intimate and meaningful relationship. Wally's line of work requires him to be out of town several days month. Upon returning from a business trip, he typically goes to see Marge at her apartment. On this visit, when Marge answers the door, Wally presents her with a dozen long-stemmed roses. Marge looks at the roses and then at Wally. Her face remains expressionless. She does not accept the flowers. Instead, she asks Wally who he was messing around with while out of town. Wally is stunned. Before he can reply, Marge pushes him toward the elevator and tells him she never wants to see him again.

This interaction can also be broken into the four components:

1. **Event:** Wally gives Marge roses.

2. **Belief:** Marge tells herself Wally was cheating on her.

3. **Emotion:** Marge feels suspicious and angry.

4. **Behavior:** Marge pushes Wally toward the elevator, telling him she never want to see him again.

Why might Marge feel suspicious and angry in the second scenario? Perhaps she received roses from a previous boyfriend after he cheated on her.

It is irrelevant whether or not Wally cheated on Marge. If he did cheat, but she interpreted receiving the roses as an indication of how much he cared for her, she would still feel happy and, consequently, give him a kiss and hug. Conversely, if Wally did not cheat on Marge, but Marge interprets the roses as an indication that he did, she will feel suspicious and angry and behave differently. Wally's motivation has nothing to do with how Marge feels or behaves—only she controls the feeling and behavior through her interpretation. Although we might understand this, few of us know how to apply this knowledge to change our feelings and behavior in our daily lives.

Remember that part of the difficulty in changing our beliefs is that beliefs attain the status of fact once we hold them. Remember also that we are often not aware of our beliefs because they become habitual. Many of the beliefs we access automatically are irrational (dysfunctional schema). They do not accurately match the situation. When this occurs, it is more likely that we will overreact emotionally and be unable to access an effective response. Therefore, it is important to recognize our irrational beliefs and combat them effectively.

Combating Irrational Beliefs

As stated in Part II, it is a human condition to engage in irrational thinking styles. Ellis believed that these irrational thinking styles stem from a hereditary predisposition and social learning

(Ellis, 1962). Let's look at the four irrational thinking styles described by Ellis and his colleagues (Dryden and DiGiuseppe, 1990):

1. **Awfulizing**—Expressing a belief that a situation is more than 100-percent bad, worse than it absolutely should be.

2. **"I can't stand it! It's awful!"** (low frustration tolerance)—Being unable to envision having any happiness at all if demand is not met.

3. **Damnation**—Being excessively critical of self, others, and/or life conditions.

4. **Always-and-never thinking**—Insisting on absolutes (e.g., that you will always fail or never be approved of by significant others) (p. 4).

In addition to these four, Ellis identified a fifth irrational thinking style:

5. **Demandingness**—Using words such as "must" and "should."

When we direct "must" and "should' towards others we are experiencing anger, frustration, and resentment. For example, saying to yourself "He *should* treat me respectfully" when a student calls you a jerk only escalates your emotions. Then you are more likely to engage in counterproductive behavior. Directing "must" and "should" at ourselves results in feeling guilty and also limits our ability to respond effectively.

Miller, who studied under Ellis, developed an innovative way of combating irrational thinking styles. He coined the following sentence, containing four of the irrational thinking styles (Miller, 1986). This sentence is sure to result in overreacting emotionally, limiting our ability to respond effectively:

That event (whatever is was) shouldn't have happened, it's awful that it did, I can't stand it, and somebody around here needs to be condemned and damned as rotten and worthless—let's see, is it me, is it you, or is it the way the world works (p.138)?

The sentence can be made specific to a given situation. For example, if a student calls you a jerk, the sentence would be: "That student shouldn't have called me a jerk, it's awful that he did, I can't stand it, and he needs to be condemned and damned."

When we think "You must and if you don't, I can't stand it," we are making others the target of our irrational thinking. When we think "I must and if I don't I won't be able to stand it," we are making ourselves the target or irrational thinking. When we think "the world must and when it doesn't, it's awful and I can't stand it," we are making the world the target of irrational thinking.

Eliminating demandingness, awfulizing, and "I can't stand it—It's awful!" reduces our tendency to condemn and damn. The key to eliminating these irrational beliefs is to interpret situations in a hard-nosed, literal, precise, and factual manner.

Demandingness

Demandingness is the most difficult thinking style to eliminate because the strategies for shifting this way of thinking go against social convention. Yet, demandingness is the major reason we overreact and exhibit counterproductive behavior. Recall that the development of schema was discussed in Part II. We develop schema to interpret new information and want our interpretations to be uniform (or consistent). Consistency breeds predictability and feelings of comfort. Therefore, we have the tendency to take information that does not fit our schema and interpret it as wrong, bad, or dangerous.

Every time we overreact, we demand something of others or of ourselves. For example, you might respond to the student who calls you a jerk by thinking, "He should not have called me a jerk." or "He needs to be more respectful." These statements demand that the student change—something you have no control over. In another example, you might make demands on yourself. For example, after criticizing a colleague in front of others, you might think, "I should have been more considerate." This statement, too, is a demand. You cannot take back the criticism. Placing demands on ourselves, others, or the world fails to acknowledge the reality of the situation. It is futile to try to change reality to the way we want it to be.

The strategy to combat demandingness is deceptively simple: Use demanding words only to describe reality. It is important to more fully understand the meaning of demanding words in order to implement this strategy.

The words in *Table 4-1* reflect demandingness. The word *must* according to the *American Heritage Dictionary* means "imperative requirement." *Must* and the other words in *Table 4-1* indicate that there is absolutely no choice involved. To eliminate demandingness, we must use these words exactly as they are defined. That is, we use these words if a situation is a *must* or

Demanding Words	
Must	Got to
Should/Shouldn't	Need to
Have to	Ought to

Table 4-1
When we use words that imply that we have no choice, we escalate our emotions.

Nondemanding Words	
Desire	Prefer
Ethics	Probably
Etiquette	Sensibilities
Expect	Values
It would be better if	Want
Morals	Wish
Practicalities	

Table 4-2
When we use words that imply that we have a choice, we do not escalate emotions.

have to, when we have absolutely no choice. We use these words when compelled by forces beyond our control to do something. If we use these words when there is any choice at all, then we are engaging in demandingness.

A simple test to determine if you are engaging in demandingness is to reexamine the definition of *must* and ask yourself, "How much choice is involved?"

Definition of must:	Imperative requirement = have to/no choice.
Example:	I must be on time for work.
Test Question:	Is it possible not to be on time regardless of the consequences?

Figure 4-1

In the example of this test given in *Figure 4-1*, we ask if it is possible to not be on time, regardless of the consequences. The answer is "yes," it is possible to not be on time for work. There is no supernatural force that takes over your body in the morning and compels you to be on time.

Using demanding words when you are late to work only escalates your emotional state. If you are driving to work after leaving the house late, thinking, "I must be on time" or "I need to be on time," you create stress for yourself. If, instead, you think, "It would be preferable to be on time" (using a nondemanding word from *Table 4-2*), you decrease your emotionality. Then you are less likely to be irritated by others who you perceive as driving slowly. If you refrain from engaging in demandingness, the demand to be on time is turned into what it really is—a preference.

In certain situations demanding words can be used factually. Some "musts" are true. If we drop a pen, it *must* fall to the ground. The guideline for using *must* or any of the demanding words is to make sure that it describes reality. Here is another example: What must we be doing right now? Reading this book. Why must we be reading this book? Because we are. How long must we read this book? Until we stop.

Here is another example. During a presentation, I drop an eraser on the floor and ask, "Where is the eraser?" The audience answers, "On the floor." I ask, "Where *must* the eraser be?" Again, the answer given is "On the floor—because it is." The next question I ask is, "Where does the eraser *need* to be?" This time the uniform answer is, "On the chalk tray." That answer is wrong. The demanding word *need* is not being used to describe reality. The correct answer is, "On the floor." The eraser *needs* to be wherever it is. Remember, we are just describing reality. The final question I ask is, "Where should the eraser be?" The audience answers again, "On the chalk tray." However, *should not* the eraser be where it is? This answer seems wrong to us. Here is why: We initially acknowledge the reality that the eraser is on the floor. No demand has yet been made. We then tell ourselves that it is not practical or sensible to keep the eraser on the floor. Again, no demand has been made. However, because it is not practical or sensible to keep the eraser on the floor (because it is not easily accessible to use

there), we make a demand. "The eraser should not be on the floor." Unfortunately, using the words *should* or *should not* has no impact on the eraser. It doesn't move off the floor and onto the chalk tray. We can look down at the eraser on the floor and say "should" repeatedly for 24 hours, and the eraser still will not magically levitate to the chalk tray.

Perhaps more than any other demanding words *should* and *shouldn't* are the most difficult to use factually. We so want to use them to change reality. Let's illustrate this tendency using a previous example: A student calls you a jerk. The first thing you tell yourself is "That student just called me a jerk." You have acknowledged a reality. However, because you do not like being called a jerk, you immediately make a demand: "He *shouldn't* have called me a jerk." This heightens your emotional level—perhaps to a point where you are unable to access effective ways of responding. Instead, it would have been more effective to say to yourself, "He *should* have called me a jerk. Why? Because he did." This statement sounds ludicrous. Yet, no amount of saying "shouldn't" will reverse time and force the student to say something polite. Furthermore, your emotions will level off. Regardless of how silly this may sound, you would gain the emotional control necessary to access an effective response. Otherwise, your feelings get in the way and you fall back on the punishment techniques that give the student exactly what he wants— power and control.

It is difficult to use demanding words to only describe reality because it is difficult to separate *acceptance* from approval. We tend to not accept something if we do not approve of it. You can eliminate this tendency by keeping in mind these three steps:

1. *Acceptance* simply means acknowledging that a reality occurred.

2. You do not have to *approve* of something in order to accept its reality.

3. Once you accept the reality of a situation, you can place it on the physical injury scale (described in the next section, "Awfulizing") and determine how bad it is.

These three steps are used in the following scenario. Suppose that you go out to your car and see that the windshield is broken. "Should the windshield be broken?" "Yes, because it is." No amount of saying "shouldn't" will repair the windshield. Saying "shouldn't" would only increase your emotional reaction. By saying, "My windshield should be broken," you automatically diminish your emotions. If the person getting into the car next to you hears you say this, she may respond by asking, "Do you like the fact that your windshield is broken?" Of course, your answer would be "No, I don't like that my windshield is broken, but I accept the reality that is." In other words, you do not have to approve of the situation in order to accept its reality. Once you accept that your windshield is broken, you can determine just how bad it is.

Awfulizing

Other terms for awfulizing are "catastrophizing," "making mountains out of mole hills," or "blowing things out of proportion." Awfulizing is a logical extension of engaging in demandingness. If you say something should or shouldn't have happened, the interpretation will be that it is awful that it did.

In order to combat awfulizing, it is important to understand and accept two fundamental assumptions. The first assumption is that 100 percent

equals all. One hundred percent means we get all of whatever it is we are talking about. It is not possible to get more than 100 percent. Therefore, it is erroneous and ludicrous when a sports announcer says that a race car driver gave 110 percent on the last lap. This statement is not grounded in reality. Every grade-school student who has learned about percentages knows you can't give more than 100 percent. The second assumption is that whenever something negative happens to us, we describe it as being bad.

Here is the logical deduction of these two assumptions:

Bad (negative) things that can happen to us range from an extremely miniscule amount of "badness" (e.g., .0000001 percent) to the

How Bad Is It?	
100%	– Death
95%	– 4 limbs cut off
90%	– 3 limbs cut off
85%	– 2 limbs cut off
80%	– Dominant arm cut off
75%	– Nondominant arm cut off
70%	– 1 hand cut off
65%	– 1 foot cut off
60%	– 3 fingers cut off
55%	– Big toe cut off
50%	– 3 broken limbs
45%	– 2 broken limbs
40%	– Dominant arm broken
35%	– Nondominant arm broken
30%	– Broken nose
25%	– Badly sprained ankle
20%	– Laceration (6 stitches)
15%	– Cut
10%	– Bruise
5%	– Small bump
1%	– Gnat bite
0%	– Nothing

Figure 4-2
Physical Injury Scale Designed to Transform Awfulizing.

maximum of 100 percent bad. Bad things cannot be more than 100 percent.

Now we are going to transform awfulizing using the physical injury scale (see *Figure 4-2*) developed by Miller (1986). The physical injury scale will help us accurately and logically determine the degree to which certain things are bad. Human tendency is to blow things out of proportion—especially when engaging in demandingness. By comparing an event to something tangible—physical injury—we can train ourselves to see things more realistically and not get so upset. If we use the physical injury scale whenever we encounter a situation that we label as "bad," we can respond emotionally in a way that correlates to the percentage on the scale. As a result, we will feel more in control and less stressed when dealing with challenging behaviors. And, we will be able to respond in ways that are more likely to obtain a desired outcome.

Imagine your purse or wallet was stolen. Think about what has been lost. You no longer have cash or your checkbook. Sentimental items like pictures are gone. Think of all the time you'll have to spend getting a new driver's license, canceling credit cards, putting a hold on checks.

Now, pretend that you can magically get back your wallet with all of its contents. However, it will cost you some level of physical injury. Look at the physical injury scale in *Figure 4-2* and decide how much it's worth to have your wallet back. Most people would not make the trade at 45 or 50 percent. That level of pain, suffering, and inconvenience would not be worth the wallet. Conversely, 1 percent may not seem commensurate with the level of hassle you'd have to go through to replace your wallet. Let's say you settle on 20 percent and trade having a laceration requiring stitches for your wallet. Of course, get-

ting stitches means waiting in the emergency room for several hours. Then the doctor gives you a shot of local anesthetic right into the laceration and stitches you up.

If you would easily trade the laceration and stitches for your wallet, then go up to 25 percent on the scale—badly sprained ankle. If, on the other hand, 20 percent was too high, move down to a point at which you would be willing to make the trade.

What if you had to go through the same process for locking your keys in the car? How much pain would you be willing to endure to have your keys back in your hands instead of dangling from the ignition?

Most people would not go higher on the scale than 20 percent for either scenario. Now let's apply this knowledge to awfulizing. When something bad happens, ask yourself "How bad is it?" If it is only 15 percent bad, then only react with emotion commensurate to 15 percent.

Of course, many people get much more upset than 15 percent if their wallets are stolen. This overreaction is easy to demonstrate. Go back to *Figure 4-2* and place a piece of paper over the physical injuries so that only the percentages are showing. Pretend this is an "emotional reaction" scale. Think of how emotionally upset you were when your wallet was stolen or you locked your keys in your car. If you had no emotional reaction that would correlate to 0 percent. The most extreme emotional reaction humans can experience correlates to 100 percent. If we are honest, most of us would say our emotional reaction ranged between 40 percent and 65 percent—clearly higher than the level of pain we were willing to trade to have our wallet or keys back in our hands. **Emotional overpayment** is the difference between how upset we get and how bad the situation really is.

You can apply the physical injury scale to any situation. Let's return to the example of the student who calls you a jerk. Ask yourself, "How bad is it?" How much physical pain would you be willing to endure to have that student not call you a jerk? Most people who work with students with challenging behaviors would not go above 10 percent on the scale. Most of us would also feel a lot more upset than 10 percent.

One final comment about the physical injury scale: You can modify it to include any hierarchy of physical pain that makes sense to you. For example, if you feel that a sprained ankle is worse than a broken nose, place the sprained ankle higher on the scale. You can also include more items. Adjust the percentages to increase by twos or fours instead of fives. The only stipulation is that the items must make sense and go up hierarchically in nature.

We now have two methods for developing emotional control. First, when something bad happens we can tell ourselves that it should have happened. This strategy prevents escalation into demandingness. Second, we can ask ourselves, "How bad is it?" We determine the percentage, combating the irrational thinking style of "I can't stand it! It's awful!"

I Can't Stand It! It's Awful!

How many times have you said "I can't stand this anymore"? Saying "I can't stand it" is a fallacy. You are living proof that you have withstood everything that has ever happened. You can withstand everything that happens except death. And, as Erickson was fond of saying, "I don't worry about dying. In fact, it will be the last thing I do." Death is the only thing we cannot withstand.

Therefore, being hard-nosed, literal, precise, and factual will lead us to accept the following statement (Miller, 1986):

I fully realize and accept the fact that I am living proof that I have stood everything that has ever happened to me. I am going to be able to stand and handle everything that is going to happen to me except the one thing that will eventually kill me (p. 72).

Using the physical injury scale also helps us accept this statement. If you can stand receiving a cut to not be called a jerk, then you can stand being called a jerk.

Putting New Thinking Styles Together

Miller (1986) combines the strategies for combating demandingness, awfulizing, and "I can't stand it! It's awful!" into this sentence:

That event (whatever it was) should have happened, and it's about ____% bad, and I can stand a ____ (p. 72).

You can make this sentence specific to any situation. For example, if a student calls you a jerk, the sentence would be: "He should have called me a jerk, and it's about 10 percent bad, and I can stand a 10."

Remember, you are not saying that you approve of, or like, being called a jerk. Your level of displeasure is expressed by the percentage you give it on the physical injury scale. Putting the event on the physical injury scale helps to keep it in perspective. How bad can being called a jerk be if you are only willing to incur a bruise? Also, once you say you can stand a bruise, you can stand being called a jerk, thereby eliminating the "I can't stand it! It's awful!"

By practicing this sentence you are likely to react with a more reasonable emotional response. If you do not overreact, you have control. You are in a better position to access effective responses for dealing with the challenging behavior.

Chapter 13

Advanced Approaches
for Managing Resistance

Implementing advanced techniques requires proficiency in techniques already described. Working together, all the techniques in this book will help build your ability to:

- Identify, analyze, and manipulate context.
- Determine the function a challenging behavior serves and identify a replacement behavior.
- Adopt new patterns of responding by being comprehensive and unfettered by convention.

There are four advanced approaches for managing resistance:

1. Paradoxical directives

2. Therapeutic metaphors

3. Reframing

4. Surprise and shock

Of all the techniques that manipulate context, **paradoxical directives** are the ultimate. Used for many decades, they may remind you of the old term "reverse psychology," but they are much more than that. **Therapeutic metaphors** are a way to embed directions through the use of stories. **Reframing** uses a student's frame of reference to elicit a desired change. The use of

surprise and shock breaks up habitual behavioral patterns. In this way, they are similar to the approaches for scrambling a routine described in Chapter 6.

Paradoxical Directives

Paradoxical directives seem to defy logic. They convey to a student that he or she can change by remaining unchanged. With this approach you will never fight with your students. Instead, you will be able to accept a student's resistance. The student is then caught in a position where resistance is cooperation. Haley (1973) described how Erickson used an analogy of trying to change the course of a river to illustrate this point:

> *If he opposes the river by trying to block it, the river will merely go over and around him. But if he accepts the force of the river and diverts it in a new direction, the force of the river will cut a new channel (p. 24).*

The point that resistance can become cooperation is an important one that deserves elaboration. Too often we inculcate students with ways of looking at the world that have worked well for us, but that may be clumsy and inappropriate from their perspective. We expect students to accept authority. Lecturing or otherwise trying to force a student to comply with your version of the world often results in resistance (Maag, 1997).

We need to remind ourselves that no two people are alike. No two people even understand the same sentence in the same way. Erickson (1962) believed that each individual brings with him or her a model of the world that is as unique as a thumbprint. To manage resistance effectively we must not try to fit students into an adult concept of what they should be. Instead, we should join them in their frames of reference. Two examples follow:

An eight-year-old boy was half carried and half dragged by his parents into Erickson's office. The parents wanted Erickson to cure the boy of bed-wetting. The boy's anger and resentment was clearly apparent. Erickson said to him:

"You're mad and you're going to keep right on being mad. You think there isn't a thing you can do about it, but there is. You don't like to see a "crazy doctor" but you're here, and you would like to do something but you don't know what. Your parents brought you here, they made you come. Well, you can make them get out of the office. In fact, we both can—come on, let's tell them to go on out... But you're still mad, and so am I, because they ordered me to cure your bedwetting. But

they can't give me orders like they give you..." (Haley, 1973, pp. 193-194).

It was clear that the boy was angry at his parents and wanted to refuse their attempts to get him to stop wetting his bed. Bedwetting may have been a way for the boy to obtain power and control—the more the parents tried to get him to stop, the more the boy resisted. However, Erickson first established rapport with the boy. He shared the boy's frame of reference of not liking being told what to do by the parents. Erickson obtained compliance by telling the boy to banish his parents. The boy could not refuse Erickson's instruction because to do so would run counter to his resistant frame of reference. Erickson laid the groundwork for a successful intervention.

For the second example of resistance becoming cooperation, let us return to the example used in Chapter 1 of Frank and Ms. Winston. Frank threw his book on the floor and refused to pick it up. This behavior was perfectly rational from Frank's frame of reference. He became oppositional in order to regain the power and control that he perceived Ms. Winston had taken. He threw the book on the floor, but he could have just as easily displayed other inappropriate behaviors. Throwing the book, or any display of inappropriate behavior, was the least important aspect of the interaction. Frank's goal was to get Ms. Winston to give him any direction so that he could refuse to follow it, thereby regaining power and control. Ms. Winston dealt with Frank's resistance in a traditional manner. By doing so, she gave Frank exactly what he wanted: power and control.

Here is an alternative approach Ms. Winston could take, considering Frank's oppositional frame of mind. After Frank says "No, I won't, and you can't make me—nobody can make me," Ms.

Winston counters by saying, "You're right, I can't make you pick up that book. I can't even make you move that book one inch." Right then, the context surrounding the situation is changed. What is Frank to say and do? If he agrees that she cannot make him pick up the book, then initial compliance has been achieved. Conversely, in order to continue being oppositional, Frank would have to say, "Yes, you can make me pick up that book!" In this case initial compliance is also obtained. Ms. Winston could continue by saying, "And I know you can't move the book one foot. You certainly can't move the book closer to your desk." In essence, Ms. Winston is building momentum for Frank to be compliant by *using his resistance.*

Ms. Winston has simply developed rapport with Frank. Rapport is not being liked or being sympathetic. It is responding using the student's frame of reference. Creating rapport made it easier for Ms. Winston to obtain her desired outcome. She makes the shift by saying, "And I refuse to let you put the book on your desk!" Ms. Winston went from agreeing with Frank (creating rapport) to refusing to let him move the book (giving him another direction). Frank was noncompliant with Ms. Winston's first direction to pick up the book. He is anticipating being noncompliant with subsequent directions. By refusing to let Frank put the book on the desk, Ms. Winston creates cooperation—regardless of Frank's behavior. If he moves the book in order to continue being resistant, then the desired goal has been achieved. If he refuses to move the book, then he is being compliant. Either way, Frank's oppositional frame of reference has been disrupted, making it easier to subsequently direct him toward the desired outcome. Ms. Winston then says to Frank, "Thank you for following my direction. I'm pleased to see

that you are being more compliant." This statement rearranges Frank's oppositional frame of reference. The impact may not be immediate, but managing resistance is not always achieved in one fell swoop. The goal is to seed ideas that will grow into future compliance.

Paradoxical directives focus on:

1. Encouraging the student to produce the maladaptive behavior at will (compliance-based).

2. Encouraging the student to avoid behaving appropriately (defiance-based).

Both types of paradoxes require analyzing and manipulating the context surrounding a behavior. In some ways paradoxical directives are similar to the previously described techniques of scrambling routine and inconvenience.

Compliance-Based Paradoxes

Compliance-based paradoxes reduce inappropriate behaviors by making them occur voluntarily. The inappropriate behavior would occur anyway, but making its occurrence predictable interrupts the pattern of behavior. In Part II, an example of sequence confusion was presented. In this example, a student was instructed to bring on anxiety 15 minutes prior to taking a math quiz. This compliance-based paradox uses **scheduling**. There are four ways to make use of **scheduling**:

1. Instruct the student to display a target behavior at a different time.

2. Instruct the student to display a target behavior at a different location.

3. Instruct the student to display a target behavior using a different topography (appearance or form).

4. Instruct the student to display more of a target behavior.

Scheduling changes the context, thereby changing the meaning, purpose, and desire for engaging in the behavior. By instructing the student to bring on the anxiety 15 minutes prior to taking a math quiz, the teacher is requiring the student to express the symptom at a different time. If the student brings on anxiety, then he is given proof that the anxiety is under his control. If he refuses to bring on the anxiety, he is also given proof that the anxiety is under his control (because he was able to avoid experiencing it). Erickson used scheduling to discipline his own children (Rosen, 1982):

> One day my son Lance came home from grade school and he said, "Daddy, all the other kids at school get spankings and I haven't even had a spanking. So I want a spanking."
>
> I said, "There's no reason to spank you."
>
> He said, "I'll give you one," and he went outside and broke one of the windows of the hospital.
>
> I said, "No, the proper thing to do is replace the pane of glass for the window. A spanking won't do that."
>
> He was disgusted and went out and broke another windowpane. He said, "Now will you spank me?"
>
> I said, "No, I will replace the windowpane," In all, he broke seven panes of glass. While he was out breaking the seventh pane, I was on the balcony of our apartment. I lined up seven of his cast-iron trucks on the railing. He came in to announce, "I broke the seventh pane of glass; now will you spank me?"

> I said, "No, replace the panes is what I'll do." Then I said, "Now, here are seven of your trucks on the railing. I'm going to start the first one rolling down the railing. I hope it will stop and not roll off, crash, and break on the sidewalk below. Oh, that's too bad! Maybe the second one will stop."
>
> He lost seven trucks. About three weeks later he came home from school very happy. I seized him, put him over my knees, and spanked him. He said, "Why are you doing that?"
>
> I said, "I seem to remember that you asked me to spank you. I didn't meet your wishes."
>
> He said, "I know better now."
>
> Of course I didn't spank him very hard. It was a token spanking.

Permission granted from *Norton* to reprint *(pp. 250-251)*.

Rosen (1982) wrote that in this example Erickson illustrated the principle he used to both discipline children and treat patients: Do not give what is asked for. Rather, give what is called for, and give it when you deem it appropriate.

In another example Erickson uses time scheduling to discipline his grandson. Erickson's grandson Douglas came into his office while Erickson was conducting a teaching seminar (Rosen, 1982):

> I told him, "Run along, Douglas," and he answered impudently, "I couldn't hear you."
>
> "Run along," I repeated, "go into the house."
>
> Douglas left, slamming the door. Obviously he didn't like that. He shouldn't have slammed the door… I would graciously ask him, for no apparent reason, "Please slam the door." I would do this while he was busy looking at a

picture book. He'd wonder why, but would obediently do it. I'd thank him and ask him to slam the door again.

He'd say, "But I want to read my book."

"Well, just slam it again," I'd insist.

He'd slam it again and pretty soon he'd inquire why I had asked him to slam the door. I'd remind him of the original slamming and say, "The way you slammed the door made me think you liked to slam doors."

His answer would be, "I really don't like to slam doors" (p. 252).

The second use of scheduling, that of changing location, is illustrated by the "do-nothing chair." This strategy requires a student to express a target behavior at a different location. Other examples of changing location include having students throw temper tantrums in the bathroom or making siblings argue outside. In these examples, the persons displaying the behavior are asked to continue but to do so in a different location. The behaviors can no longer be performed the way they once were because the context, which originally served as a cue, has been changed.

Topography refers to physical aspects of behavior. For example, a student who throws a book is displaying three aspects of topography: body part (arms), motion (arm going forward), and object (book). Changing any aspect of topography while otherwise instructing the student to continue performing the behavior will change the context, meaning, purpose, and desire:

> A therapist worked with a 14-year-old boy with obsessive-compulsive disorder (OCD). The boy's chief complaint was that he would never be able to play basketball again because his eyes were damaged. He told the therapist that his eyes were damaged by being frequently compelled to look up at the ceiling and move his eyes from left to right seven times. The therapist told him that there was nothing he could do to fix his eyes or to help him stop engaging in this behavior. The therapist then changed the topic of conversation and asked the boy what type of books he liked to read. The therapist then told the boy to purchase a thin paperback and keep it in his back pocket. The therapist told the boy that whenever he felt compelled to look up and move his eyes to read the book instead. He told the boy that this would not cure his ritual, but would at least enable him to read more.

The paradoxical instruction to read the book while engaging in the ritual changed the meaning of the behavior. A behavior is compulsive when: (1) the person knows the compulsion is irrational and (2) the person nevertheless feels helpless to control it. If the boy is able to read the book while engaging in the ritual, he is given proof that he can, in fact, control the behavior—he has already changed an aspect of it. Conversely, if the boy refused to change the ritual, then he would also have proof of his control because he chose to behave as usual.

Erickson used a change in topography to help a mother treat her son who had a bad case of acne (Rosen, 1982):

> *"My son's a student at Harvard and he has an extremely bad case of acne. Can you treat that with hypnosis?"*

> *I said, "Yes. Why bother bringing him to me? How are you going to spend Christmas vacation?"*

She said, "I usually take a vacation from medical practice and go to Sun Valley and ski."

I said, "Well, this Christmas vacation, why don't you take your son with you? Find a cabin and remove all the mirrors in it. You can eat your meals in that cabin, and be sure that you keep your hand mirror in the safety pocket of your purse."

They spent the time skiing and the son couldn't see a mirror. His acne cleared up in two weeks time (p. 87).

In this example, Erickson changed the boy's focus of attention by removing an object that was topographically associated with acne—mirrors. There are demonstrable physical effects on the skin associated with mental imagery. The most obvious example is blushing when we think about an embarrassing situation. This approach reflects Paracelsus' declaration in the fifteenth century: "As man imagines himself to be, so shall he be, and he is that which he imagines" (p. 88).

When we have a student engage in more of a behavior, we are using the paradoxical approach of **negative practice** (described in Part II). Another term for negative practice is **ordeal therapy**. **Ordeal therapy** is based on the premise that if we make it more difficult to display a behavior than to give it up, the person will give up the behavior. The goal is to impose an ordeal that is more severe than the problem. Haley (1984) described four characteristics of a "good" ordeal:

1. **The ordeal should cause distress equal to or greater than that caused by the troubling behavior.** For example, a student who is distressed by compulsively sharpening pencils 25 times a day may be required to sharpen pencils 50 times a day at a pencil sharpener in a remote part of the school.

2. **The ordeal should be good for the person.** For example, requiring an adolescent who wants to quit smoking to keep a pack of cigarettes in a place that is only accessible by walking one mile. This would provide her with exercise.

3. **The ordeal must be something the person can do and to which he cannot legitimately object.** For example, the student who writes "School stinks" agrees to write it numerous times since it is a behavior in which she can, and wants to, engage.

4. **The ordeal should not harm the person or anyone else.** For example, a student who kicks other students or cuts himself with a knife should not be required to engage in more of these behaviors.

Haley (1973) described a 16-year-old girl who sucked her thumb to the exasperation of her parents, her teachers, her schoolmates, the school bus driver, and everyone who came in contact with her. Even the school psychologist was exasperated, telling the girl her thumbsucking was an aggressive act. Here's how Erickson used ordeal therapy to treat the thumbsucking:

The girl came unwillingly to the office with her parents. She was nursing her thumb noisily. I dismissed her parents and turned to face the girl. She removed her thumb sufficiently to declare she didn't like "nut doctors."

I replied, "And I don't like the way your parents ordered me to cure your thumbsucking. Ordering me, huh! It's your thumb and your mouth, and why can't you suck it if you want to? Ordering me to cure you! The only thing I'm interested in is why, when you want to be aggressive about thumbsucking, you don't really get aggressive instead of piddling around like a baby that doesn't know how to suck a thumb aggressively. What I'd like to do is tell you how to suck your thumb aggressively enough to irk the hell out of your old man and your old lady. If you're interested, I'll tell you. If you aren't, I'll just laugh at you."

The use of the word "hell" arrested her attention completely she knew that a professional man ought not to use that kind of language to a high-school girl... Challenging the inadequacy of her aggressiveness, a term the school psychologist had taught her, commanded her attention still more.

The offer to teach her how to irk her parents, referred to so disrespectfully, elicited even more complete fixation of her attention... Then in an intent tone of voice, I said, "Every night after dinner, just like a clock, your father goes into the living room and reads the newspaper from the front page to the back. Each night when he does that, go in there, sit down beside him, really nurse your thumb good and loud, and irk the hell out of him for the longest 20 minutes he has ever experienced."

"Then go in the sewing room, where your mother sews for one hour every night before she washes dishes. Sit down beside her and nurse your thumb good and loud and irk the hell out of the old lady for the longest twenty minutes she ever knew."

"Do this every night and do it up good. And on the way to school, figure out carefully just which crummy jerk you dislike most, and every time you meet him, pop your thumb in your mouth and watch him turn his head away. And be ready to pop your thumb back if he turns to look again."

"And think over all your teachers and pick out the one you really dislike and treat that teacher to a thumb pop every time he or she looks at you. I just hope you can be really aggressive" (pp. 195-196).

In this example, Erickson created rapport by using the girl's oppositional frame of reference and then required her to engage in the problematic behavior deliberately and to absurd lengths. The girl could not legitimately object to his request because he was asking her to do what she was already doing. However, thumbsucking would be eliminated if she chose to resist his request—hence, the paradoxical nature of the intervention.

Haley (1973) described a similar approach in which Erickson told a child that the thumb alone was not sufficient and that he should sit by his parents and suck not only the thumb but each finger as well. Erickson would often have a child watch the clock and require him to suck the thumb and fingers for a certain length of time. Thumbsucking loses its appeal when it is transformed into an ordeal.

The six stages of ordeal therapy that Haley (1984) described are summarized in *Table 4-3*. This table provides information for generating effective and appropriate ordeals to manage student resistance. Note that Stage 2 focuses on getting a commitment to overcome the problem. Although commitment helps, most students with challenging

The Six Stages of Ordeal Therapy	
Stage	**Description**
Stage 1	Clearly define the problem. Analyze the function the behavior serves and identify replacement behaviors. Because the student receives a consequence (i.e., the ordeal) whenever the problem occurs, it is best to define the problem clearly.
Stage 2	The student must be committed to getting over the problem if he or she is to follow-through with an ordeal. Help motivate the student to take this kind of drastic step.
Stage 3	Select an ordeal. Emphasize that you are not going through the ordeal. The student should be made aware that he or she is the only one with the inconvenience.
Stage 4	The directive must be given with a rationale. Give the directive clearly and precisely, so there is no ambiguity. Make it clear that the task is to occur only with the problematic behavior, and that there is a set time for engaging in it.
Stage 5	The ordeal continues until the problem behavior is resolved. The ordeal must be gone through precisely, at the precise time, and must continue until the behavior disappears. Typically the contract should be lifelong.
Stage 6	The ordeal is in a social context. Problematic behavior is a symptom within the social organization of the student. Analyze the function the behavior serves and provide a replacement behavior.

Table 4-3
How the process of ordeal therapy unfolds.

behaviors will not commit to changing—it would counter their oppositional frames of reference and the power and control they obtain. As we can see from the previous example, Erickson did not obtain a commitment to change, but rather challenged the girl to become better at sucking her thumb. This stance resulted in the girl becoming *committed* to getting better at sucking her thumb and, consequently, compliant in following Erickson's directions.

Defiance-Based Paradoxes

Defiance-based paradoxes convey to students that in order to change, they must either stay the same or give up. The idea is to have students oppose your directive. By doing so, students become compliant. The example of how Ms. Winston dealt with Frank is a defiance-based par-

adox. Defiance-based paradoxes can be delivered through:

1. The "slow down" directive (delaying change)

2. The "giving" in directive (forbidding change)

3. The relapse prediction (predicting a relapse)

4. Hard restraining (declaring hopelessness)

The "Slow Down" Directive

One way to deliver a defiance-based paradox is to give a "slow down" directive (have the student move through the intervention more slowly than he or she would normally expect). For example, you might say, "Today, it is important not to do anything to improve your behavior." Fisch, Weakland, and Segal (1982) described the importance this strategy plays in the intervention:

The client is not instructed to do anything, certainly nothing specific. Whatever instructions are given are general and vague: "This week, it would be very important not to do anything to bring about further improvement." More of the intervention consists in offering believable rationales for "going slow": that change, even for the better, requires adjusting to; or that one needs to determine, a step at a time, how much change would be optimal as opposed to maximal: "You might be better off with a 75 percent improvement rather than a 100 percent improvement"; or "Change occurring slowly and step by step makes for a more solid change than change which occurs too suddenly" (p. 159).

The "slow down" directive works paradoxically by enhancing a student's sense of control and confidence. Moving more quickly is a way to continue being oppositional (Anderson and Stewart, 1983). This technique is particularly useful for students whose approach has been to try too hard, and for students who press for urgent solutions while remaining passive and uncooperative.

The "Giving In" Directive

Another way to deliver a defiance-based paradox is to forbid the student to change the behavior. For example, you could say, "In order to find out how bad your behavior is, just give in to it and let it happen." This directive is called "giving in" (Watzlawick et al., 1974). Another example of this directive is "In order to get some information about your problem, I want you to do something new this week. Give up trying to stop arguing and then pay attention to what is happening before and during this time." Another example of

the "giving in" directive is to tell a student directly not to engage in the desired behavior. For example, a student who has been particularly resistant to completing assignments might be told, "I don't want you to complete any work today." The effectiveness of this directive can be enhanced by preceding it with the statement "It is very important that today you follow my direction to the letter." A student who is severely oppositional typically knows when you have been unsuccessful in getting compliance. The student is highly reinforced by the resulting power and control. Therefore, after hearing your first statement, the student will be even more invested in proving that you cannot get him or her to follow a direction. Eagerly awaiting your instruction, the student will listen closely in order to do the opposite of your request.

When you then say, "I don't want you to complete any of your assignment today," the student is caught in a double bind. You have built the student's resistance. Then you request that he or she do exactly what is already being done. Even if the student figures out your goal and says, "Hey, you can't fool me with that reverse psychology stuff," you still have compliance. The student is following your instruction. You have nothing to lose with this strategy because the student already has been refusing to complete work. If the student follows your instruction and does not do the work, you can say at the end of the lesson, "Thank you for following my direction today and being so compliant. I know now that it is possible for you to follow other directions and not be as resistant." This statement will cause a lot of rearrangement in the way the student is thinking. We may not have compliance at the end of the first lesson, but we have seeded the idea. We have set up future compliance. If the student wants to continue being resistant, he or she must complete the assignment.

The Relapse Prediction

The third way to deliver a defiance-based paradox is to predict a relapse. This approach can be used frequently and is an essential ingredient of most paradoxical instructions. For example, after forbidding change you might say to the student who just completed the assignment, "I want to let you know that you probably won't complete future assignments." This creates another double bind. A defiant student may want to prove you wrong by not relapsing, demonstrating that the behavior is under his or her control. Conversely, if the student fails to complete another assignment, he or she is also being compliant, demonstrating that the behavior is under control.

Predicting a relapse can also be used when terminating a successful intervention. Simply tell the student that it is normal and expected for the problem to reappear. If the problem reappears, then it is under your control, making future attempts more successful. If the problem does not reappear, then the student has proof that it is under his or her control.

Hard Restraining

The fourth way to deliver a defiance-based paradox is to declare hopelessness—that is, to predict that change is not possible. For example, you could say "I think it is really impossible for you to finish your homework." This approach called "hard restraining" is the most extreme. In hard restraining, you present an attitude of resignation and then challenge the student to prove you wrong. It is important that you do not project the feelings of hopelessness on the student. You do not want the student to think that you think he or she is hopeless—only that the change in behavior is hopeless.

Hard restraining should only need to be used infrequently. Most students will respond to the "slow down" directive or giving in directive. Reserve hard restraining for students who perceive their behavior as out of their control—who want help, but fail to improve. When called for, you might say something like, "I know I originally made a mistake in assuming we could work together to help you become less anxious. I now know that I can't really offer you anything at this point that will improve your predicament. It would be wrong of me to continue trying. Instead, it would probably be best for you to learn to live with the anxiety." At that point, in order for the student to remain resistant, he or she would have to say. "That's a crock. Of course you can help me. After all, you're the teacher!" This resistant response actually gains compliance. On the other hand, if the student agrees, then rapport has been created because his or her world view is congruent with yours. Then it becomes easier to move the student in the direction of a desired outcome because of mutual agreement.

Table 4-4 provides a summary of the seven steps described by Cormier and Cormier (1985) for working paradoxically. These steps require careful timing and delivery and should be offered with warmth and empathy. Be genuinely pleased that the student has the opportunity to get "really good" at the problem behavior. Avoid sarcasm and displaying anger.

Cautions When Working Paradoxically

Use paradoxical techniques, or context manipulations, to engender compliance, but keep in mind that they are no panacea. There are situations in which paradoxical techniques are not appropriate.

	Steps	**Description**
		The Seven Steps of Working Paradoxically
1	Therapeutic Relationship	Paradoxical directives work best when a student is actively involved in the intervention and a supportive, therapeutic relationship exists.
2	Assessment	Paradoxical directives are more effective when functional assessment is conducted first. Failure to base paradoxical directives on functional assessment often creates difficulties because contributing contingencies are overlooked.
3	Goals	Base paradoxical directives on the direction and degree of change desired by the student. Carefully delineate the student's reasons for performing the behavior so that you are not pursuing the wrong outcome.
4	Formulation	Formulate paradoxical directives by (1) considering the problem in functionally positive terms, (2) understanding how the problem is perpetuated and maintained, and (3) hypothesizing the function that the problem serves for the student.
5	Assignment	Assignment of the paradoxical directive can be the most crucial and difficult part of the intervention. Reserve assignment until after several sessions to avoid mistaking the function. Giving the directive later in the process prevents the student from commenting on it, increasing its effectiveness. Provide a rationale that will motivate the student.
6	Evaluation	Monitor the results of the paradoxical directive. Record the type of task given and track its effects. Note whether the effects were similar to or different from those you expected.
7	Follow-up	Successful changes must be nurtured and solidified. Nonparadoxical techniques, including reinforcing the new behavior, are helpful.

Table 4-4

As you progress through each step, continue to convey warmth and empathy.

Avoid using paradox with students who have strong self-doubts or pose a danger to themselves or others. Also avoid using paradoxical techniques with students with antisocial or paranoid tendencies. They may change the task to fit their own needs or may become suspicious.

Because paradoxical techniques are unorthodox and rely on some deception, they may appear to violate the ethical principle of informing students of the rationale and technique. However, if a paradoxical technique is based on an accurate functional analysis, it is possible to openly tell a student why a task is being assigned.

Paradoxical interventions are often complex and require ample skill and energy to implement them

effectively. It's important to not present or use them in a cavalier fashion. Although many educators use paradoxical techniques intuitively and quite successfully, there are ethical and legal ramifications to their use. For example, you may set up a place and time for a student who repeatedly uses foul language to "practice swearing." This technique may be effective, but the student's parents may find it objectionable and, consequently, pursue legal action. If you use this technique, be sure to obtain parental permission first.

Potential problems can be avoided by conducting functional assessments prior to implementing paradoxical interventions. In this capacity, paradoxical techniques can be used to test hypotheses regarding the intent of behavior.

Therapeutic Metaphors

We've all had the experience of hearing a story in which the characters are grappling with a conflict that we ourselves are trying to solve. The story immediately becomes significant to us (Gordon, 1978). We become curious about the story's resolution.

These stories become **therapeutic metaphors** when they instruct or advise the listener. By telling a story to a student, you can provide guidance without raising the student's anxiety level. The student can then assimilate the information without becoming resistant. When you express ideas in metaphors, students will interpret what they hear in terms of their own experiences. Erickson successfully used therapeutic metaphor to treat bed-wetting (Haley, 1973):

A mother called me up and told me about her ten-year-old son who wet the bed every night. They had done everything they could to stop him. They dragged him in to see me—literally. Father had him by one hand and mother by the other, and the boy was dragging his feet. They laid him face down in my office. I shoved the parents out and closed the door. The boy was yelling.

When the boy paused to catch his breath, I said, "That's a goddamn hell of a way to do. I don't like it a damn bit." It surprised him that I would say this. He hesitated while taking that breath, and I told him he might as well go ahead and yell again. He let out a yell, and, when he paused to take a breath, I

let out a yell. He turned to look at me, and I said, "It's my turn." Then I said, "Now it's your turn," so he yelled again. I yelled again, and then said it was his turn again. Then I said, "Now, we can go right on taking turns, but that will get awfully tiresome. I'd rather take my turn by sitting down in that chair. There's a vacant one over there." So I took my turn sitting down in my chair, and he took his turn sitting down in the other chair. That expectation had been established—I had established that we were taking turns by yelling, and I changed the game to taking turns sitting down. Then I said, "You know, your parents ordered me to cure you of bed-wetting. Who do they think they are that they can order me around?" He had received enough punishment from his parents, so I stepped over on his side of the fence by saying that. I told him, I'd rather talk to you about a lot of other stuff. Let's just drop this talk about bed-wetting. Now, how should I talk to a ten-year-old boy? "You're going to grade school. You've got a nice compact wrist. Nice compact ankles. You know, I'm a doctor, and doctors always take an interest in the way a man is built. You've got a nice rounded, deep chest. You're not one of these hollow-chested, slump-shouldered people. You've got a nice chest that sticks out. I'll bet you're good at running. With your small-sized build, you've undoubtedly got good muscle coordination." I explained coordination to him and said he was probably good at sports that required skill, not just beef and bone. Not the sort of stuff that just any bonehead could play. But games that require skill. I asked what games he played, and he said, "Baseball, and bow and arrow." I asked, "How good are you at archery?" He said, "Pretty good." I said, "Well, of course that requires eye, hand, arm, body coordination." It turned out his younger brother played football, and was larger than he, as were all the other family members. "Football's a nice game if you've got just muscle and bone. Lots of big, overgrown guys like it."

So we talked about that and about muscle coordination. I said, "You know, when you draw back on your bowstring and aim your arrow, what do you suppose the pupil of the eye does? It closes down." I explained that there were muscles that are flat, muscles that are short, muscles that are long—and then there are muscles that are circular, "like the one at the bottom of your stomach; you know, when you eat food that muscle closes up, the food stays in your stomach until it's all digested. When the stomach wants to get rid of the food, that circular muscle at the bottom of your stomach opens up, empties out, and closes up to wait till the next meal to digest." The muscle at the bottom of your stomach— where's the bottom of your stomach when you're a small boy? It's all the way down.

So we discussed that for an hour, and the next Saturday he came in all alone. We talked some more about sports and this and that— with never a mention of bed-wetting. We talked about Boy Scouts and camping, all the things that interest a small boy. On the fourth interview he came in wearing a big,

wide smile. He said, "You know, my Ma has been trying for years to break her habit. But she can't do it." His mother smoked and was trying to stop. I said, "That's right, some people can break their habits quickly, others make a great big talk about it and don't do nothing about it." Then we drifted on to other subjects.

About six months later he dropped in socially to see me, and he dropped in again when he entered high school. Now he's in college.

All I did was talk about the circular muscle at the bottom of the stomach closing up and holding the contents until he wanted to empty it out. Symbolic language, of course, but all that beautiful build-up of eye, hand, body coordination. The bed-wetting went away without ever discussing it (pp. 199-201).

The most important aspect of a therapeutic metaphor is that it utilizes a student's model of the world. The content does not necessarily have to match the student's situation, but it does have to preserve the structure of the student's problematic situation. In other words, the salient factors of the metaphor are the student's interpersonal relationships and the patterns within the context of the problem. In the previous example, Erickson did not talk about bed-wetting. He talked about muscle structure and coordination, and sports. However, the salient factor—the importance of exerting "muscle control" was preserved and stressed.

Constructing Metaphors

There are three steps for constructing an effective metaphor; although Gordon (1978) stated that construction does not always require you to follow each step:

- Structural equivalence
- Thoroughness
- Workable resolution

Metaphors need to satisfy a basic pattern requirement (i.e., the habitual ways a student responds). They must be structurally equivalent with the problem situation, must be developed thoroughly, and must provide a workable resolution that is therapeutically effective and sufficient.

Structural equivalence refers to the degree of similarity between the student's experiences and those portrayed in the metaphor. You can increase the relevance, thoroughness, and resolution of a metaphor by including these four components:

1. The problem should be well-formed.

2. Characters and events should be equivalent to individuals and events that characterize the student's situation or problem.

3. The metaphor should resolve the problem.

4. The metaphor should represent a connecting story.

These components are included in the following metaphor told by a teacher to help a student stop snooping:

"And in this forest community there lived an anteater named Wag. Now Wag, of course, had a long nose. This didn't bother her, but she could see that it was often the focus of attention in the forest, which did sometimes bother her. When a squirrel came up to admire her nose she narrowed her eyes and snobbishly said, "Isn't is obvious that you should be nut-gathering now, instead of this wool-gathering?"

In this example, it is likely that the student will recognize the metaphorical connections between her snooping and Wag's nose. If she takes offense or is bored by the obvious story connections, it may jeopardize the story's therapeutic effectiveness. However, the story can still be effective if the metaphor is relevant to the student. The relevance and significance of a metaphor is increased when the problem is well-formed, the characters and events are equivalent to those reflected in the student's actual situation, and when the metaphor resolves the problem.

1. **The problem should be well-formed.** Obtain a thorough understanding about the nature and characteristics of the problem. In what ways (if any) does the student want to change his or her situation? Here is an example of a well-formed metaphor:

   Sally missed the volleyball team bus that was going to the meet in a town two hours away. She stomped up to the school secretary and loudly demanded that someone from school drive her to the meet. Hoping to appease her, the secretary told her that she would see what she could do. Sally was obviously pleased and expecting "action." The secretary was lying in order to quiet Sally down. A few minutes later the secretary returned, commiserated with Sally, and assured her that there was no one at school who could drive her. She said Sally should be at the bus earlier next time. Sally then called the secretary a foul name.

From this story we see that Sally had a problem and that the secretary probably did want to help her. Their interaction, however, was bound for disaster because Sally settled on an unrealistic goal as the solution to her problem. The secretary then tacitly accepted that goal. Sally's problem was ill-formed. Its solution involved events and/or people over which neither she nor the secretary had control.

Ill-formed goals frequently occur when working with students with challenging behaviors. The student wants you to "make George leave me alone" or "make Nancy like me." Although such requests represent desirable outcomes, they are beyond your control and are, therefore, often long and fruitless attempts at change. It is not that such goals are impossible to reach. But, if they are attained, it is because the student has made changes rather than changing the behaviors of others. Having well-formed goals is a prerequisite for an effective therapeutic metaphor. The changes to be made are changes over which the student has control.

Creating Events in a Therapeutic Metaphor		
Actual Situation		**Metaphorical Situation**
Principal is not available.	➡	Captain is shut up in cabin.
Student gets into trouble.	➡	Cabin Attendant sets the wrong sails.
Teacher covers for principal.	➡	First Mate corrects the Cabin Attendant and tries to reset sails.
Student walks out of room.	➡	Cabin Attendant goes to galley.
No resolution, problem recycles.	➡	Problem recycles until . . . resolution.

Figure 4-3
How a situation can be represented in therapeutic metaphor.

2. **Characters and events should be equivalent to individuals and events that characterize the student's situation or problem.** Include each significant person in the cast of characters. Also represent the situation and processes involved in the metaphor. These representations may not "be equal" to the parameters of the problem, but they should be "equivalent" in the sense that they maintain the same relationships. Let us assume that the student gets upset because the principal is not available to talk when he gets into trouble. The teacher tries to handle the situation. This only further infuriates the student. In *Figure 4-3* a boat is chosen as a context for the metaphor. Three people involved in the student's problem are transformed into the "protagonists." The characters have the same relationships as the actual individuals *(Figure 4-4)*.

There are no limitations on the situations that can be depicted or the types of characters that can be included in therapeutic metaphor. The transformations are concerned only with relationships in the previous example; we could have just as easily selected for the characters a pair of schooners and a sailboat; two trees and a sapling; or a stallion, a mare, and a colt.

3. **The metaphor should resolve the problem.** The resolution depends on the desired outcome. You may have to rely on your personal intuitions regarding which changes in behavior might be most useful for the student. However, in many cases, the student determines the resolution. Often, the student knows the changes needed. Where they get stuck is in building the bridge from their present, unsatisfactory, recurring problem to the desired outcome. For example, a student may tell you that he or she wants to deal with the

Creating Characters in a Therapeutic Metaphor		
Actual Situation		**Metaphorical Situation**
Principal	→	Captain
Teacher	→	First Mate
Student	→	Cabin Attendant

Figure 4-4
How key people can be represented in a therapeutic metaphor.

problem without walking out of the room, but does not know how. This problem is very common. At some time in our lives we have all been so close to the trees that we have missed the forest. One function of a metaphor is to provide the student with a way to step back and take a look at the "forest." The two components of resolution are a desired outcome, and a strategy that bridges the gap between the problem and the desired outcome.

4. **The metaphor should represent a connecting story.** Often the student has been trying unsuccessfully to jump from the problem to the new behavior. The metaphor must offer a bridge. Like the outcome, the connecting strategy is usually implied in the student's own description of the situation. Sometimes it may be inherent to the relationship between the problem and the desired outcome. You could devise several possible strategies capable of helping the student control his or her temper and not leave the classroom. For example, the student could ask why you are taking over for the principal. Ultimately though, the best strategy is the one that the student either directly or indirectly indicates. To get this informa-

tion, ask the student to describe in detail how he or she has tried to solve the problem in the past. In describing the failure, the student will describe what needs to be done to reach the goal. You'll be informed by the description of the points at which the student gets stuck and of how his or her ability is limited.

Let's say the student in the example tells you that she is trying to tell you that she needs to see the principal. The student also tells you she does not believe you have the ability to solve the problem. She believes she would be wasting her time to stay in the classroom. The connecting strategy in this case might be to tell the student what type of help you can give and what knowledge and skills you possess that can help. With this strategy, you can complete the metaphor:

> The Cabin Attendant set wrong sails. The First Mate sees this, walks over, and tries to correct him. The Cabin Attendant asks the First Mate if she knows how to set sails. She replies that she has been setting sails for several years and learned how to do so directly from the Captain. The Cabin Attendant then tells the First Mate that he needs help tying the half-hitch knot. The First Mate responds by showing the Cabin Attendant how to tie this knot.

Strategies for Telling Metaphorical Stories

Gordon (1978) described many strategies for effectively telling metaphors, including:

- Covert versus overt metaphors
- Fairytales versus anecdotes
- The use of quotes
- Guided fantasies

It is not always necessary to play down the fact that a metaphor is intended to be therapeutic. It is not even necessary that the student be unaware of the connections between the real situation and significant people and those in the metaphor. One of the primary functions of a therapeutic metaphor is to provide the student with the opportunity to step back, out of the trees, and take a look at the forest. Erickson accomplished this goal using a therapeutic metaphor with a patient who was an alcoholic (Rosen, 1982):

Usually I send alcoholic patients to AA because AA can do a better job than I can do. An alcoholic came to me and he said, "My grandparents on both sides were alcoholics; my parents were alcoholics; my wife's parents were alcoholics; my wife is an alcoholic and I have had delirium tremors eleven times. I am sick of being an alcoholic. My brother is an alcoholic too. Now, that is a hell of a job for you. What do you think you can do about it?"

I asked him what his occupation was.

"When I am sober I work on a newspaper. And alcohol is an occupational hazard there."

I said, "All right, you want me to do something about it—with that history. Now, the thing I am going to suggest to you won't seem the right thing. You go out to the Botanical Gardens. You look at all the cacti there and marvel at cacti that can survive three years without water, without rain. And do a lot of thinking."

Many years later a young woman came in and said, "Dr. Erickson, you knew me when I was three years old. I moved to California when I was three years old. Now I am in
Phoenix and I came to see what kind of a man you were—what you looked like."

I said, "Take a good look, and I'm curious to know why you want to look at me."

She said, "Any man who would send an alcoholic out to the Botanical Gardens to look around, to learn how to get around without alcohol, and have it work, is the kind of man I want to see! My mother and father have been sober ever since you sent my father out there."

"What is your father doing now?"

"He's working for a magazine. He got out of the newspaper business. He says the newspaper business has an occupational hazard of alcoholism."

Now, that was a nice way to cure an alcoholic. Get him to respect cacti that survive three years without rain. You see you can talk about your textbooks. Today you take up this much. Tomorrow you take up that much. They say you do such and such. But actually you ought to look at your patient to figure out what kind of man he is—or woman—then deal with the patient in a way that fits his or her problem, his or her unique problem (pp. 80-81).

Covert Metaphors

Erickson's metaphor was an example of indirect suggestion applied symbolically. Whether a student responds best to overtly communicating the metaphor's significance or not depends on the student's temperament.

Covert metaphors are seemingly unrelated to the student's life. In the example of Ms Winston and Frank, a covert metaphor is used: Recall that Frank threw his book on the floor and refused to pick it up and return to his chair. Ms. Winston used a paradox. She told Frank not to pick up the book. In order to be resistant, Frank had to pick up the book. However, he may have tried to outsmart Ms. Winston by saying, "Hey, you're trying to use that reverse psychology stuff on me, and it won't work!" He then stood defiantly unmoving. But in this case, Frank is still being compliant with the direction. Ms. Winston could respond by thanking him for following her direction. Now she has an opening. Frank is momentarily being compliant and his oppositional frame of reference is disrupted. Ms. Winston tells Frank a story:

> "You know, Frank, as you stand there following my direction, it reminds me of a childhood friend of mine, Freddy. He was in the Boy Scouts. Out of all the activities in Boy Scouts, Freddy really liked the weekend camping outings. He liked most of all being in the tent and playing card games. He also like sitting around the campfire. However, he really disliked helping to set up the tent and gathering the firewood. This would sometimes be a problem for Freddy because when he refused to set up the tent, the scoutleader would not let him play games inside the tent. And when Freddy refused to help gather firewood, he was not allowed to sit by the campfire and roast marshmallows at night. Sometimes Freddy disliked helping so much that it was worth it to him not to play cards in the tent and sit by the campfire. But, at other times, he would help so that he could participate in the two camping activities he enjoyed most.

Covert metaphors, often called "My friend John" metaphors, are simply a retelling of the student's problem, with an added resolution, told as though it were a problem "someone else" had and solved. In this example, two messages are conveyed to Frank. The first message is that there is nothing wrong with refusing to follow directions. However he must decide whether not following directions is worth the consequences. The second message conveyed in the metaphor is that Frank is capable of making decisions and that although following directions may not be fun, there are personally advantageous consequences for doing so.

Overt Metaphors

In contrast to covert metaphors, **overt metaphors** directly relate to the student and his or her problem. For example, a student that is having difficulty dealing with a peer's teasing may be told a story about how to handle this problem. The advantage of overt metaphors is that they are easy for the student to identify. The disadvantage is that they are easy for the student to identify. In essence, the same feature (easy to identify) is an asset and a liability. The asset is that the student will understand what you are trying to do. The liability is that this direct approach can create resistance. Covert metaphors address this problem. Four types of covert metaphors follow:

1. Fairytale metaphors

2. Anecdotes

3. Using quotes

4. Guided fantasies

1. **Fairytale metaphors** are characterized by their extraordinary occurrences and characters or by endowing inanimate objects with human emotions. Do not be too quick to dismiss telling fairytales to adolescents or young adults. A well-told fairytale can be as compelling and effective as a contemporary story (Gordon, 1978). Adolescents and young adults

do not necessarily find fairytales insipid. In our own lives we are sometimes blessed by seemingly divine resolution of a conflict. Sometimes we meet special or bizarre characters. Sometimes we talk to our cars or computers.

2. **Anecdotes** are brief fairytales cast within the context of everyday life. Anecdotes usually need to be delivered covertly so that the connection to the student's real life does not raise resistance.

3. **Using quotes** is a third strategy for telling metaphors. You can covertly make direct suggestions to students by dressing up the statement as a quote made by someone else. This approach allows you to make a direct statement without claiming personal responsibility for the statement's content. For example, you might be working with a student who uses foul language. To make the point that this type of language is not only disrespectful, but also will not get the student what he or she wants, you could use the quote approach:

A student came running in one of the teacher's rooms and said "Where the hell's the pencil sharpener?" The teacher told him that talking in a disrespectful way will not get his question answered. If he wanted to rephrase his question more politely, then the teacher would answer it.

Or you could personalize the quote if you think it could have more impact.

A student came running in my room and said "Where the hell's the pencil sharpener?" I told him that talking in a disrespectful way to me will not get his question answered. If he wanted to rephrase his question more politely, then I would answer it.

A student can argue with you and discredit statements you make, but can do little about things said by "someone else." In this approach, you simply have the characters in the story say what it is you want to say.

4. **Guided fantasies** are metaphors that students construct and use. What could be more meaningful than a metaphor you construct yourself? Guided fantasies allow students to pursue a fantasy, directed by your comments and questions. In this way significant aspects of the fantasy can be attended to. Guided fantasies can be made more effective by incorporating other metaphor strategies. For example, you can modify a guided fantasy by turning over the responsibility for solving the problem in the metaphor to the student. The student finishes the metaphorical fairytale that you begin. This modification is particularly effective with

elementary students because they are usually very attentive to stories, readily accept the reality of the characters, and easily generate creative solutions (Gordon, 1978).

The covert metaphor approach can be particularly effective within the unfinished metaphor. In this modification, you would describe the situation of a child or friend who has a similar, or even identical problem to the student's problem, feigning ignorance of what to do (which, considering the problems of some students, may not require feigning). Then ask the student what he or she would do about the situation. The student's answer is a blueprint for solving the real problem because it came from his or her own model of the world. It may not even be necessary to further develop from that blueprint because students often realize at this point that they have just solved their own problem.

Reframing

Reframing is an important part of using metaphors. The meaning of a situation and its corresponding behaviors depends on the frame of reference in which they are perceived. Bandler and Grinder (1982) illustrated this point with a story:

An old Chinese Taoist story describes a farmer in a poor country village. He was considered very well-to-do because he owned a horse which he used for plowing and for transportation. One day his horse ran away. All his neighbors exclaimed how terrible this was, but the farmer simply said "Maybe."

A few days later the horse returned and brought two wild horses with it. The neighbors all rejoiced at his good fortune, but the farmer just said "Maybe."

The next day, the farmer's son tried to ride one of the wild horses; the horse threw him and broke his leg. The neighbors all offered their sympathy for his misfortune, but the farmer again said "Maybe."

The next week conscription officers came to the village to take young men for the army. They rejected the farmer's son because of his broken leg. When the neighbors told him how lucky he was, the farmer replied "maybe . . ." (p. 1).

Changing a student's frame of reference changes the meaning and purpose of the behavior, and the desire to engage in it. This approach, called **reframing**, involves modifying the student's perceptions or views of a situation or behavior. Reframing is not new to the therapeutic process. Anyone who tries to get students to "think about things differently," "see a new point of view," or "take other factors into consideration" is attempting to reframe. Reframing also occurs in fairy tales and fables: the ugly duckling turns out to be a swan and Rudolf the Reindeer's funny-looking red nose becomes a useful beacon for guiding Santa's sleigh on a foggy night (Bandler and Grinder, 1982).

Therapeutically, reframing focuses on the meaning of a behavior or its context. Every experience and every behavior is appropriate, in a specific context or frame of reference. Much of the behavior viewed as resistance is indicative of an internal context and set of past experiences in which the behavior is inappropriate. If you say to a student, "You really did a great job completing your math problems," and the student responds with "Fine, but I don't really care. I didn't do that good of a job, so I wish you wouldn't lie to me," that is a pretty good indication that the student is operating out of a unique internal frame of reference. Upon further exploration, you might find that the student believes compliments mean doing more work or that teacher demands will increase. If a behavior seems bizarre or inappropriate, we are really just failing to appreciate the context the behavior is based on. You can use the two types of reframing—meaning reframing and context reframing—to help your students change their behaviors.

Reframing Meaning

Meaning reframing challenges the meaning assigned to the problem behavior. When a student attaches a particular meaning to a behavior, it becomes necessary for maintaining consistency and predictability. The longer the meaning is attached to the behavior, the more the student is likely to see things in only one way or from one perspective. Meaning reframing provides alternative views of a problem behavior without directly challenging the behavior itself. It loosens the entrenched frame of reference. For example, a student's "stubbornness" might be reframed as "independence." "Greed" might be reframed as "ambition."

The major goal of meaning reframing is to help students make sense of their ongoing experiences with respect to their personal models of the world. Gordon and Meyers-Anderson (1981) provided the following example of how Erickson used a meaning reframe to help a client with insomnia:

> Insomnia is your misuse of time . . . those are bonus hours. While you are awake in bed start thinking about all of the pleasant things that you want to do, that you have done, and you'll find that they are bonus hours, not insomnia hours. So you'll find

> yourself with thoughts of something pleasant, your body will become accustomed to the bed, and you'll go to sleep (p. 58).

"Insomnia is your misuse of time . . . those are bonus hours." With these few words, Erickson reorients the client with respect to the problem, so that what seemed an encumbrance is suddenly revealed as a mitigation. This contrary interpretation of insomnia is much more than simple word play. It is a shift in perspective that made it possible for Erickson to help the client to have more useful bedtime experiences.

Bandler and Grinder (1982) described how therapist Leslie Cameron-Bandler used meaning reframing to treat obsessive-compulsive disorder house cleaning:

> The rest of the family could function pretty well with everything the mother did except for her attempts to care for the carpet. She spent a lot of her time trying to get people not to walk on it, because they left footprints—not mud and dirt, just dents in the pile of the rug.

> When this particular woman looked down at the carpet and saw a footprint in it, response was an intense negative kinesthetic gut reaction. She would rush off to get the vacuum cleaner and vacuum the carpet immediately. She was a professional housewife. She actually vacuumed the carpet three to seven times a day. She spent a tremendous amount of time trying to get people to come in the back door, and nagging at them if they didn't, or getting them to take their shoes off and walk lightly.

> What Leslie did with this woman is this: she said "I want you to close your eyes and see your carpet, and see that there is not a single

footprint on it anywhere. It's clean and fluffy—not a mark anywhere." This woman closed her eyes, and she was in seventh heaven, just smiling away. Then Leslie said "And realize fully that that means you are totally alone, and that the people you care for and love are nowhere around." The woman's expression shifted radically, and she felt terrible! Then Leslie said "Now, put a few footprints there and look at those footprints and know that the people you care most about in the world are nearby." And then, of course, she felt good again (pp. 5-6).

In this example, Cameron-Bandler does not try to change the stimulus (i.e., the obsessive-compulsive cleaning tendencies). Instead, the meaning of having a clean carpet is reframed. There is nothing inherently bad about the stimulus (cleaning). The client made a judgment that footprints on the carpet were important enough to feel bad about. Cameron-Bandler redefined the footprints as being important enough to feel good about, changing the response of the client (Bandler and Grinder, 1982).

One teacher used meaning reframing with a 17-year-old student who returned from suspension for fighting. The student explained that his fights occurred because other guys were talking to his ex-girlfriends. When asked what this meant, he replied that the boys were disrespecting him. The teacher and student then discussed, with enormous grandiosity, his prowess in attracting beautiful girlfriends—how he always broke up with them and never got dumped, and how any girl would be thrilled to date him. The teacher then turned to the student and said "Maybe when some guy is talking to an ex-girlfriend that means he *respects* your taste in women." This meaning reframe was acceptable to the student for two rea-

sons. First, it focused on the importance the boy placed on being "disrespected," reorienting the interaction to "respect." Second, the reframe fed into the student's adolescent male ego regarding his perceived desirability. In the future, seeing some guy talk to an ex-girlfriend might serve as a reminder that he is desirable to females, thereby lessening the urge to respond aggressively.

Reframing Context

In addition to reframing the meaning of a behavior, the context can also be reframed. Reframing the context helps students decide when, where, and with whom a given problem behavior is useful or appropriate (Bandler and Grinder, 1982). In essence, **context reframing** helps students answer the question "In what place in your life is a particular behavior useful and appropriate?"

Context reframing is based on the assumption that every behavior is useful in some, but not all, contexts or situations. Thus, when a student says, "I won't do my assignment," the context could be reframed by asking, "In what situations, or with what people, is it useful or even helpful not to do what an adult asks?" Two situations immediately come to mind: being solicited by an adult to try a drug; and being asked to get into a stranger's car.

Bandler and Grinder (1982) provided the following example of a context reframe used by noted family therapist Virgina Satir:

Virgina was working with a family. The father was a banker who was professionally stuffy. He must have had a degree in it. He wasn't a bad guy; he was very well-intentioned. He took good care of his family, and he was concerned enough to go to therapy. But basically he was a stuffy guy. The wife was an extreme placater in

Virgina's terminology. A placater is a person who will agree with anything and apologize for everything. When you say "It's a beautiful day!" the placater says "Yes, I'm sorry!"

The daughter was an interesting combination of the parents. She thought her father was the bad person and her mother was the groovy person, so she always sided with her mother. However, she acted like her father.

The father's repeated complaint in the session was that the mother hadn't done a very good job of raising the daughter, because the daughter was so stubborn. At one time when he made this complaint, Virgina interrupted what was going on. She turned around and looked at the father and said "You're a man who has gotten ahead in your life. Is this true?"

"Yes."

"Was all that you have just given to you? Did your father own the bank and just say 'Here, you're president of the bank'?"

"No, no. I worked my way up."

"So you have some tenacity, don't you?"

"Yes."

"Well, there is a part of you that has allowed you to be able to get where you are, and to be a good banker. And sometimes you have to refuse people things that you would like to be able to give them, because you know if you did, something bad would happen later on."

"Yes."

"Well, there's a part of you that's been stubborn enough to really protect yourself in very important ways."

"Well, yes. But, you know, you can't let this kind of thing get out of control."

"Now, I want you to turn and look at your daughter, and to realize beyond a doubt that you've taught her how to be stubborn and how to stand up for herself, and that that is something priceless. This gift that you've given to her is something that can't be bought, and it's something that may save her life. Imagine how valuable that will be when your daughter goes out on a date with a man who has bad intentions" (pp. 8-9).

In this example, being stubborn was viewed by the father as a bad trait in the context of the parent-child relationship. However, being stubborn becomes good in the context of dating a man with bad intentions. The context used to evaluate the behavior was changed. The father might then be less likely to view his daughter's stubbornness as disrespect because in a different context it might keep her safe.

Context reframing can be used for many problem behaviors. For example, it would be difficult to use a paradoxical technique for stealing, but you could reframe the context. You wouldn't want to tell students to steal more or to steal at a different time or place. Instead, a context reframe can be an effective intervention. There are many skills and traits necessary to be a successful thief, including being observant, organized, meticulous, strategic, quick, and evasive. These skills are employed to target the object, plan the theft and escape route, and decide what to do with the object (e.g., keep it or sell it). A detailed risk assessment must be conducted to avoid being caught. Avoiding being caught requires discretion. Creativity is essential to generating a plausible alibi. These skills can be positively reframed in the contexts of professions: educator, therapist, business person, politician. In the case of a student who steals, you could reframe the skills in a positive context:

> "You know, you've become pretty good at stealing. You obviously are very observant, organized, meticulous, strategic, quick, and evasive. I think we can use those skills. I've noticed that we often lose many things here at school: pencils, paper, student projects, cleaning supplies, and such. I think you could help us find these items without anyone else knowing what you're doing. Also, I think your skills could help me keep track of how many visitors enter the school. We have to know who's coming and going and people don't always remember to go to the office and sign in. I'd like you to help me keep track of people visiting the school."

Reframing the context provides the student with appropriate ways to obtain attention (assuming that gaining attention was the function of the behavior).

The Five Steps of Reframing

Five steps can help you use reframing effectively (Gordon and Meyers-Anderson, 1981). These steps are based on determining the cause of the behavior or what is preventing a more appropriate behavior from occurring. By making this determination you can identify the secondary gain of the behavior. For example, in the case of fighting with peers, the primary gain is to stop teasing. The secondary gain is obtaining respect from tough peers. The five steps of reframing identified by Gordon and Meyers-Anderson (1981) are:

1. Identify the cause-effect relation as perceived by the student.

2. Identify the highly valued, desirable state connected to the target behavior (in the student's perspective).

3. Develop rapport by explicitly stating your understanding of the cause and effect of the student's problem (as perceived by the student).

4. Get the student to commit to defending his or her present perspective.

5. Make explicit the cause-effect relation between the student's target behavior and the highly valued, desirable state.

Let's apply these five steps to the example of the student who got into fights whenever someone talked to his ex-girlfriends.

The first step is to identify the stated or supposed cause-effect relation between the target behavior (fighting) and the student's desired goal (respect). That is, what does the student believe to be the cause of his difficulties? In this example, the student believed that the cause of his aggression was the other boys talking to his ex-girlfriends.

Step 2 involves identifying the highly valued and desirable state that the student believes is connected to his behavior. In this example, the student identified two states: respect and desirability to women.

In Step 3, rapport is developed by explicitly stating your understanding of what the student identified as being the cause and effect of the problem. Success rests on your ability to get the student to accept your version of reality. I cannot overstate the importance of building rapport. In the example, rapport was built through discussing with much grandiosity the student's ability to attract girlfriends.

In Step 4, the student commits to defending his present perspective. By engaging the student in an inflated and egotistic dialogue, the scene is set for the new frame of reference that will shortly be offered. By first getting the student to solidly commit to his position of being desirable, the reorientation process can be more thorough.

Step 5 involves presenting the new perspective. It is very important to give the impression that you believe what you are saying. If the student believes your communication is insincere, it will be ignored. In the example, the new perspective that the boys indicated their respect for the student when they talked to his ex-girlfriends was presented as the teacher's belief.

Rosen (1982) provided an example of Erickson using meaning reframing in which the five steps are easily identifiable:

One day a college girl passes flatus loudly in the classroom while writing on the blackboard. She turned and ran out and went to her apartment, drew the blinds, and ordered her groceries over the telephone and collected them long after dark. And, I got a letter from her saying, "Will you accept me as a patient?"

I noticed the Phoenix address that she gave and I wrote back, "Yes, I would." And she wrote back, "Are you really sure you want me as a patient?" I wondered about it—and I wrote back, "Yes, I would like you."

It took her about three months, and then she wrote me and said, "I would like an appointment with you after dark. And I don't want anybody to see me. Now, please don't have anybody around when I come to your office."

I gave her a ten-thirty appointment, and she told me about passing flatus loudly in the classroom and running out of the room and confining herself to her cabin. She also told me that she was a converted Catholic. Now, converted Catholics are always so ardent; and I questioned her, "Are you really a good Catholic?" And she assured me she was. And I spent a couple of hours with her, questioning her about her goodness as a Catholic.

And then in the next interview, I said, "You say you are a good Catholic. Then why do you insult the Lord; why do you make a mockery of him? Because you are. You ought to be ashamed of yourself—making a mockery of God and calling yourself a good Catholic!" She tried to defend herself.

I said, "I can prove that you have little respect for God." I hauled out my anatomy book, an atlas, showing all the illustrations of the body. I showed her a cross-section of the rectum and anal sphincter.

I said, "Now, man is very skilled at building things. But, can you imagine a man being sufficiently skillful to build a valve that contains solid matter, liquid matter, and air—and emits downward only the air?" I said, "God did. Why don't you respect God?"

Then I told her, "Now, I want you to demonstrate earnest, honest respect for God. I want you to bake some beans. They are called whistleberries by the navy. Flavor them with onions and garlic. And get in the nude and prance and dance around your apartment, emitting loud ones, soft ones, big ones, little ones . . . and enjoy God's work."

And she did that. A year later she was married and I made a house call to check up on her. She had a baby. And while I was visiting her, she said, "It's time to nurse the baby." She opened her blouse, exposing her breast, and fed the baby and chatted casually with me. A complete change of reference.

Note. From *My Voice Will Go With You: The Teaching Tales of Milton H. Erickson (pp. 151-152)* by Milton Erickson and Sidney Rosen, M.D. Copyright © 1982 by Sidney Rosen, M.D. Used by permission of W.W. Norton & Company, Inc.

Gordon and Meyers-Anderson (1981) made the following analysis of this reframe in relation to the five steps. Erickson did not reassure the client that there was nothing wrong with flatulence in front of others. To do so would have destroyed rapport because her belief was to the contrary (recall the discussion in Part II about matching an individual's pessimism with pessimism). The client believed that her having passed gas in class in some way made her unsuited to be in public. The consequence of this belief was her reclusive behavior. Erickson selected something out of the client's model of the world about which she had very strong, highly valued feelings—her belief in the sanctity of God and her religion. It is important to note in this example that Erickson first satisfies himself that the belief is highly valued before using it as the catalyst for the reframe. He made certain that the client was sincere in her respect for God's work before moving to the next step. Then he had the client extend those respectful feelings to her rectum. Erickson identifies the client's initial beliefs as to cause-effect (i.e., "passing gas in class makes me unfit to be in public") and identifies a highly valued content area with which her unwanted behavior can be

connected (i.e., respect for God's work). He then gets the client to defend her position as someone who has respect for God's work. Polarizing the client's beliefs in this way serves to make the revelation of God's engineering a dramatic and powerful experience. Erickson then described how flatulence is a demonstration of God's handiwork rather than a shameful lack of control as she had believed. For this client this new perspective turned a serious breech of etiquette into an opportunity for reverence, making it possible for her to rejoin society.

Gordon and Meyers-Anderson (1981) observed that Erickson did not instruct the client to continue and amplify the symptom (paradoxical directive). In this case, Erickson reoriented the client so that her flatulence became something worthy of respect and, therefore, learned to respond to it differently and control it as well.

Surprise and Shock

Surprise and shock disrupt rigid mental sets. The unexpected always serves to dissipate resistance. Never do the expected! Here is how Erickson used surprise and shock to treat the destructive behavior of a 12-year-old girl (Rosen, 1982):

At Worcester Hospital, the superintendent remarked one day, "I wish somebody could find some way of handling Ruth."

I inquired about Ruth, a very pretty, petite twelve-year-old girl, very winning in her ways. You couldn't help liking her. She was so nice in her behavior. And all the nurses warned every new nurse who came to work there, "Keep away from Ruth. She'll tear your dress; break your arm or your foot!"

The new nurses didn't believe that of sweet, winsome twelve-year-old Ruth. And Ruth would beg the new nurse, "Oh, would you please bring me an ice-cream cone and some candy from the store?"

The nurse would do it and Ruth would accept the candy and thank the nurse very sweetly, and with a single karate chop break the nurse's arm, or rip her dress off, or kick her in the shins, or jump on her foot. Standard, routine behavior for Ruth. Ruth enjoyed it. She also liked to tear the plaster off the walls periodically.

I told the superintendent I had an idea, and asked if I could handle the case. He listened to my ideas and said, "I think that will work, and I know just the nurse who'll be glad to help you."

One day I got a call. "Ruth is on a binge again." I went to the ward. Ruth had torn the plaster off the walls. I tore off the bed clothes. I helped her destroy the bed. I helped her break windows. I had spoken to the hospital engineer before going to the ward; it was cold weather. Then I suggested, "Ruth, let's pull that steam register away from the wall and twist off the pipe." And so I sat down on the floor and we tugged away. We broke the register off the pipe.

I looked around the room and said, "There's nothing more we can do here. Let's go to another room."

And Ruth said, "Are you sure you ought to do this, Dr. Erickson?"

I said, "Sure, it's fun, isn't it? I think it is."

As we walked down the corridor to another room there was a nurse standing in the corridor. As we came abreast of her, I stepped over and ripped her uniform and her slip off so she stood in her panties and bra.

And Ruth said, "Dr. Erickson, you shouldn't do a thing like that." She rushed into the room and got the torn bedsheets, and wrapped them around the nurse.

She was a good girl after that....

Note. From *My Voice Will Go With You: The Teaching Tales of Milton H. Erickson (pp. 229-231)* by Milton Erickson and Sidney Rosen, M.D. Copyright © 1982 by Sidney Rosen, M.D. Used by permission of W.W. Norton & Company, Inc.

Erickson's intervention certainly was unconventional and may even be questioned ethically. However, previous efforts to get Ruth to stop destroying property and tearing nurses' clothes were ineffective. Ruth's aggressive behavior was definitely dangerous to others. Traditional isolation approaches such as time-out didn't work. Ruth might have found isolation reinforcing because she could use her inappropriate behavior to escape or avoid undesirable tasks. Isolation also did not provide Ruth with opportunities to learn and practice appropriate ways of accomplishing her desired outcome.

Erickson had nothing to lose because the staff was unable to get Ruth to stop destroying property and tearing clothes. Therefore, one more piece of destroyed property and another torn piece of clothing would not have an appreciable impact on the hospital budget.

The intervention worked because Erickson showed Ruth what her behavior was like. Often, students can be shocked out of performing inappropriate behaviors.

Surprise and shock makes use of schemas (see Part II). You may recall that schema are information sets that help us interpret, or make sense of, new experiences. They also guide our behavior. We usually try to attach the simplest and most functional schema to a situation—a process referred to as **elegance** (Bandler and Grinder, 1975). An elegant interpretation of a situation is one that requires the minimum number of schema.

We can use the principle of elegance to surprise or shock students into compliance. When a schema is disrupted, students are momentarily left without a plan of action. It is at this precise moment that they are open to following directions. Bandler and Grinder (1975) illustrated how Erickson used the surprise and shock approach to induce a hypnotic trance using a standard handshake. A handshake is a complex pattern of behavior that is carried out at the unconscious level. Through repetition it has become automatic. When someone extends her hand, you automatically access the handshake schema which tells you to extend your hand, clasp her hand, and move them up and down together several times. But what would happen if, as you extended your right hand in greeting, the other person grabbed your wrist with her left hand and raised your arm so that it was parallel with your shoulder? At that moment, your handshake schema is interrupted. You are left momentarily with no schema to guide your behavior. Consequently, you are more likely to follow whatever instruction is given at that moment.

Here is a unique way a first-year teacher used surprise and shock to diffuse a confrontation with a student. The teacher was nervous as she called roll. When she finished she asked if there were any students whose names had not been called. A tough-looking boy in the back of the class, wearing jeans and a T-shirt with a pack of cigarettes

rolled up in one sleeve, leaned back in his chair. He looked up from cleaning his fingernails with his pen knife and said, "Yeah, you didn't call my name." "And what is your name?" inquired the teacher. The boy looked at her and said, "*@!# you." There was a sound of students taking deep breaths. Then a hush fell over the room as the students looked back and forth from the teacher to the student. Without changing her expression the teacher replied, "Is 'You' your first or last name?" This unexpected response caught the student off guard and diffused his desire to be confrontational. It is when we do the unexpected that we rearrange a student's thinking.

Hassenpflug (1983) described how she used surprise and shock successfully after trying everything else:

On that day when all the classroom management systems I had diligently absorbed in years of inservices completely collapsed, I tried insanity. As I approached the classroom, students were not doing what they were supposed to be doing, and the noise level reached an ear-piercing volume. I refused to start screaming or shouting commands and threats. I simply walked into the room, looked down at the floor as if addressing a small dog, and said, "Toto, I don't think we're in Kansas anymore." As students began to turn toward me to see what was going on, I asked one of the worst offenders if he would like to take Toto out into the hall to play for a while. More heads turned and more mouths shut.

The noise and activity were still out of control, though, so I called for the ward nurse and inquired about the name of the asylum from the inmates of the room. While waiting for her arrival, I talked to an imaginary elf (but a stuffed animal or small statue would have done as well) about the unbelievable behavior of these students. When I ran out of conversation, I started watching an imaginary wasp flying around the room. Almost everyone's eyes were on the teacher now. One particularly nasty individual, however, was still putting on a show of his own. I took my clipboard and stood by him and silently noted down everything he did as if I were an entomologist studying a new species.

Shortly, this student was so fed up that he sat down without my ever having to say a word. I sauntered over to another offender and began speaking politely in a mixture of French and German. The student turned red and sat down. Class was ready to begin now, and the preliminary calming procedures had taken only five minutes in comparison to the usual ten to fifteen of yelling.

My first attempts at insanity were so successful that I added new absurdities to my repertoire. To the student reeking of garlic who seemed to be constantly leaning on my desk and rearranging my papers, I announced that my desk had been contaminated with poison ivy. Although I was immune, I feared she might not be. She immediately backed away, and, whenever she ventured closer, I just smiled and said my magic phrase, "poison ivy."

Another girl regularly stood by my desk and whined about not wanting to work. She always demanded to know why she could not be sent to the gym instead. One day, I jumped up, slammed down my book, and walked out

of the room. Upon my return in about two minutes, she was doing her assignment and never again asked to go to the gym.

On especially bad days, I just stopped talking to students altogether. Instead, I wrote commands on large sheets of paper or on the blackboard. I wrote individual notes to offenders as well, and they usually stopped talking to read their notes and then got on with the work. To divert the class's attention from ongoing incidents of misbehavior, I began pointing out the window and describing all the imaginary beings, events, and objects I saw out there. When a particularly obnoxious student started asking me questions about the assignment before I was ready to begin giving directions, I ignored the person and talked about the spaceship waiting outside for us. I gave the student the desired attention, but I hadn't allowed myself to be forced to dance to his or her tune.

For long-lasting effect, I developed an imaginary creature known as Dragon Lady. Misbehaving students started getting notes from Dragon Lady delivered to their homerooms. The notes commanded individuals to do such things as return library books, stay awake during a movie, and stop bullying another student or face Dragon Lady's wrath. Dragon Lady periodically left her pencil or her paw print in the classroom as additional evidence of her existence (pp. 33-34).

Teachers and mental health workers are not the only people who can effectively use surprise and shock. Parents are equally adept at using this approach. A school counselor told me that her friend was very good at using this approach when her daughter would tantrum. Her daughter pitched a fit in the middle of the mall one day. It was a real floor-mopping tantrum—the child was screaming and rolling around on the floor vigorously flailing her arms and legs. Instead of being embarrassed because others were observing the scene, the mother responded by immediately dropping to the floor screaming and flailing her arms and legs. Her daughter immediately stood up and said "Mom, stop it!"

Many techniques of surprise and shock use humor to get a change in behavior. Humor can be effective as long as it does not embarrass the student and is not couched in sarcasm. Sarcasm is a display of anger. When we are sarcastic, a student knows that we are angry. We are giving the student power and control because we are showing that he or she was able to "push our buttons."

The effects of humor have been studied for hundreds of years. In the last two decades, researchers have found that humor relaxes body systems and creates feelings of well-being. Humor also defuses tense situations and creates a climate conducive to teaching and learning. A humorous comment can penetrate a tense and anxiety-producing situation. If used judiciously and without intent to put down or embarrass students, humor is an effective way to manage resistance.

Humor can be found in almost anything, even things that are not inherently humorous. Professional comedians make us laugh about divorce, unemployment, phobias, poverty, insecurity, and even death. Well-placed humor takes the sting out of pain, making new or frightening situations more palatable.

Erickson understood the usefulness of humor in coping with setbacks and unpleasant surprises.

Gordon and Meyers-Anderson (1981) described how Erickson not only used his own infectious sense of humor effectively but was able to instill in his clients a similarly lighthearted perspective:

I had an alcoholic woman who came to me for therapy . . . and she was telling me the troubles she was having with her college-aged daughter. She said, "I've had trouble with her ever since she went riding in our convertible. We were having a happy time and a bird flying overhead happened to make a deposit just when she was yawning. And she's been so ashamed with herself ever since. She just can't seem to face life at all. And my alcoholism doesn't help her."

I said, "Well, tell me a few more things about your daughter." "She's really a very nice girl, but she's awfully neurotic on that one subject." "Does she ever have a sense of humor?" The mother said, "Yes, but not since then." She had developed a lot of food avoidances that made her life very miserable.

I asked the mother, "You said she has a good sense of humor but she hasn't used it for a few years. Well, you must have a lot of humor dammed up behind that capable person. So do you mind if I do a little therapy long distance?" The mother said, "No, I don't mind." So I mailed the girl a postcard from Philadelphia advising her about the perils of yawning while riding in a convertible.

The girl got that card and said, "Who is that man and how did he ever find out about it? I know I never told him. Did you tell him?" She said, "What's his name?" The girl said, "It's signed M.H. Erickson." And the mother said,

"I've never been to Philadelphia. I don't know of anybody who lives in Philadelphia by that name. Isn't it rather a funny thing?"

The girl burst into laughter and said, "It certainly is." And she laughed, oh, uproariously

for quite some time. And resumed normal living. It was just friendly advice.

Note. From *Phoenix: Therapeutic Patterns of Milton H. Erickson* by Gordon, D. and Meyers-Anderson, M. (1981) pp. 29-30. Capitola, CA: Meta. Reprinted with permission.

Conclusion

Three riddles were presented at the beginning of Part I to help us see things from alternative perspectives:

1. What has four wheels and flies?

2. What is green all over and has wheels?

3. What do Alexander the Great and Smokey the Bear have in common?

Here are the answers:

1. A garbage truck.

2. Grass. I lied about the wheels.

3. They have the same middle name.

Many of us know the answer to the first riddle. The answer to the second riddle is impossible to solve using any traditional paradigm. The answer to the last riddle contains a visual cue—the word "the." However, our paradigms do not usually let us see the "the." We instead ponder what a conqueror and a symbol of forest fire prevention have in common. On the other hand, if the riddle was worded as "What common word do the two proper nouns Alexander the Great and Smokey the Bear have in common," then the answer would be perfectly clear. What is obvious from one paradigm can be imperceptible in another.

Five concepts presented throughout this book form a foundation for a paradigm shift. This shift focuses on becoming better observers of behavior so that we can alter our behavior to obtain desired outcomes. The five core concepts are:

1. Understanding the difference between knowledge and knowing.

2. Creating rapport.

3. Using resistance to obtain compliance.

4. Manipulating context.

5. Determining the function of behaviors.

Understanding the Difference Between Knowledge and Knowing

We have much more knowledge than we let ourselves know. Paradigm paralysis does not permit us to see our options. We tend to follow a careful routine, limiting our patterns of responding. In addition, we often are afraid to do something unconventional because it may not work. Numerous examples of breaking with convention appear throughout this book: Erickson stomped on the feet of the patient with catatonic schizophrenia, I asked participants to open their fists rather than trying to pry them open, the mother dropped to the floor and flailed her arms and legs to stop her daughter's tantrum. All of these responses were unfettered by convention.

You can more easily obtain a desired outcome when you consider all the options. However, it is important to remember that not every strategy will work every time with every student. There is no panacea for managing resistance. Managing resistance will be a futile endeavor if we view it only as the application of specific intervention strategies. Instead, we must continually alter our communication patterns. If what we are doing is not working, then we need to try something else. This phrase, so easy to understand, is difficult to put into practice. To do so, we must take a risk. The risk of trying something new and failing is so often viewed as more aversive than continuing to respond in ways that don't work. We lose sight that trying and failing is not failing—it is assessment. Never trying something different is failing. Students will always communicate how we can deal with them effectively. The key is to carefully observe their behaviors and alter our responses until we achieve the desired outcome.

Creating Rapport

Rapport permits us to more easily move a student in the direction of the desired outcome. Contrary to popular belief, rapport does not focus on conveying genuine, unconditional regard, empathy, and honesty. It is not the ability to be sympathetic, and it is not being liked. There is nothing wrong with conveying sympathy and interacting pleasantly, but these interactions do not create rapport. Rapport means observing a student's verbal and nonverbal behavior and responding symmetrically to what he or she presents.

Numerous examples of developing rapport were proffered throughout this book. Two examples are particularly illustrative: the case of Frank and Ms. Winston and the case of the student who was afraid to fail his math quiz. Ms. Winston responded to Frank's resistance by saying "You're

right, I can't make you pick up that book. I can't even make you move that book one inch." That statement built rapport. Frank and Ms. Winston were congruent. Then Ms. Winston initiated the move toward the desired goal by saying, "I refuse to let you move that book to your desk." This statement was paradoxical because Frank's behavior—regardless of what course of action he chose—was redefined as cooperation.

In the second example the student said "I know I'm going to flunk my math test and I'm scared." The response, "You're probably going to flunk this test very badly, and it's best to be scared," was congruent with the student's pessimistic frame of reference. Then movement to the desired outcome was initiated: "I bet there have been math tests in the past that you almost flunked." This statement began the process of examining whether or not the student's belief was accurate.

There will be times when you may create resistance instead of rapport. Developing rapport is a skill that is continually refined throughout our lives. Rapport is fluid. It would be foolish to think that once rapport is created that it will be maintained forever without any further work. Therefore, we must constantly adjust our behavior based on the behavior our students present to us. Through practice, rapport becomes easier to acquire and maintain.

Using Resistance to Obtain Compliance

Recall that resistance is generated from your behavior. Students communicate how to deal with them effectively. When a student says "You can't make me," he is telling you how to use his resistance. Respond by saying, "You're right, I can't make you, and I refuse to let you...." Don't be afraid of resistance. The more resistant we perceive a student to be, the easier it is to obtain compliance. The key is to not take students' challenging behaviors personally. All too often when a student says, "You can't make me," we treat it as a threat to our authority. We then are the ones who create a power struggle, thereby giving the student exactly what he or she wants. We cannot make a student do anything. We can try to influence, but we cannot make.

Techniques for controlling our emotions can help us not take behavior personally so that we can access alternatives to manage resistance. To be successful, we must respond in the direction of the resistance. For example, if you ask a student to walk outside and she says, "I'm going to run," the last thing you want to say is "You better walk!" Instead, accept her response, even encourage it, by saying, "That's fine, you can run even faster and farther." This approach puts the student in a situation in which her attempt to resist is defined as cooperative behavior. The student must follow your direction, no matter what she does. Once the student is cooperating, she can be diverted into new behavior. Rarely do we want to tell a student to stop what they are doing—unless the behavior is dangerous to self or others. Tell students to do what they are already doing, but then interject some difference. This approach is based on the idea of manipulating context.

Manipulating Context

Changing the context of a behavior sets in motion a domino effect. The meaning a student holds for the behavior, the purpose of the behavior, and the desire to engage in the behavior change. Numerous examples of this sequence (depicted in Figure 1-4) were provided, including the woman who hoarded towels and the "do-nothing chair."

Context can be changed by instructing the student to continue engaging in the behavior but interjecting a small difference. Have the student do more of the behavior, or engage in the behavior at a different time, location, or topography. Having a test-anxious student bring on the anxiety 15 minutes before entering the classroom is an example of changing the time. The "do-nothing chair" is an example of changing the location. Having a student scream while also jumping up and down is an example of changing the topography.

This book was replete with examples of how to change the context surrounding a behavior to reduce resistance. However, changing the context alone is insufficient. A student will simply begin performing another inappropriate behavior that shares the same function. It is therefore important to examine the function a behavior serves.

Determining the Function of the Behavior

All behavior is purposeful and serves some function. Students behave intentionally in order to obtain a desired outcome or goal. They may not always be consciously aware of their desired outcome though. Sometimes their behavior and thoughts have become automatic through habitual use. The outcomes desired are always appropriate and normal. Reasons for behavior include obtaining power/control or attention, and escaping/avoiding. There is nothing deviant about any student wanting to attain these outcomes. However, problems arise when students display inappropriate behaviors to accomplish these goals.

When we determine the function the inappropriate behavior serves, we can then teach a replacement behavior. Students are less likely to engage in inappropriate behaviors when we give them replacement behaviors to accomplish the same goals.

To determine the function, we can manipulate context and see if the behavior persists. Assigning a high-interest task will help us determine if the function is escape/avoidance. Determining the function is not difficult if we adopt a mindset of "thinking outside of the box." Therefore, another riddle may be an appropriate ending to this book:

> *There is a Persian story of a father who dies, leaving his earthly belongings (consisting of 17 camels) to his three sons. The instructions left specify that the eldest son is to receive one-half, the second son one-third, and the youngest son one-ninth of the camels. No matter how the sons try to divide the camels, they do not equal the fractions. Eventually, a mullah comes along on his camel, and they ask him for help. "There is nothing to it," he says. "Here, I add my camel to yours, which makes 18. Now you, the eldest, receive one-half, which is nine. You, the middle son, are entitled to one-third, which is six; here they are. You, the youngest, get one-ninth, that is two camels. This leaves one camel, namely, my own." Having said this, the mullah gets on his camel and rides off.*

References

Preface

Cormier, W.H. & Cormier, L.S. (1985). *Interviewing strategies for helpers: Fundamental skills and cognitive behavioral interventions* (2nd ed.). Monterey, CA: Brooks/Cole.

Haley, J. (1993). *Jay Haley on Milton H. Erickson*. New York: Brunner/Mazel.

Walker, H.M., Colvin, G. & Ramsey, E. (1995). *Antisocial behavior in school: Strategies and best practices*. Pacific Grove, CA: Brooks/Cole.

Part I: The Nature of Rapport

Ayllon, T. (1963). Intensive treatment of psychotic behavior by stimulus satiation and food reinforcement. *Behavior Research and Therapy, 1*, 53-61.

Bandler, R. & Grinder, J. (1975). *Patterns of the hypnotic techniques of Milton H. Erickson, M.D.* (Vol. 1). Capitola, CA: Meta.

Coren, S., Porac, C., and Ward, L.M. (1984). *Sensation and perception*. Orlando, Fl.: Harcourt.

Erickson, M.H. (1975). Varieties of double bind. *American Journal of Clinical Hypnosis, 17*, 143-157.

Gordon, D. & Meyers-Anderson, M. (1981). *Phoenix: Therapeutic patterns of Milton H. Erickson*. Cupertino, CA: Meta.

Haley, J. (1993). *Jay Haley on Milton H. Erickson*. New York: Brunner/Mazel.

Kuhn, T.S. (1970). *The structure of scientific revolutions* (2nd ed.). Chicago, IL: University of Chicago Press.

Maag, J.W. (1997). Managing resistance: Looking beyond the child and into the mirror. In P. Zionts (Ed.), *Inclusion strategies for students with learning and behavior problems* (pp. 229-271). Austin, TX: Pro-Ed.

Maag, J.W. (1999). *Behavior management: From theoretical implications to practical applications*. San Diego: Singular Press.

Neel, R.S. & Cessna, K.K. (1993). Behavioral intent: Instructional content for students with behavior disorders. In K.K. Cessna (Ed.), *Instructionally differentiated programming: A needs-based approach for students with behavior disorders* (pp. 31-39). Denver, CO: Colorado Department of Education.

Rogers, C. (1951). *Client-centered therapy*. Boston:Houghton-Mifflin.

Rosen, S. (1982). *My voice will go with you: The teaching tales of Milton H. Erickson*. New York: Norton.

Rossi, E.L., Ryan, M.O. & Sharp, F.A. (Eds.). (1983). *Healing in hypnosis: The seminars, workshops, and lectures of Milton H. Erickson* (Vol. 1). New York: Irvington.

Zeig, J.K. (Ed.). (1998). *Ericksonian psychotherapy* (p. viii). New York: Brunner/Mazel.

Part II: From Child to Context

Azrin, N.H., Nunn, R.G. & Frantz, S.E. (1980). Habit reversal vs. negative practice treatment of nervous tics. *Behavior Therapy, 11*, 169-178.

Bandler, R. & Grinder, J. (1975). *Patterns of the hypnotic techniques of Milton H. Erickson, M.D.:* Vol. 1., Capitola, CA: Meta.

Beyer, J.K. (1976). Conducting moral discussions in the classroom. *Social Education, 40*, 194-202.

Ellis, A. (1984). Rational-emotive therapy. In R.J. Corsini (Ed)., *Current psychotherapies*, (3rd ed., pp. 196-238). Itasca, IL: Peacock.

Erickson-Elliott, Erickson, L., Erickson, A., Erickson, R. Erickson-Klein, R. & Erickson, K.K. (1985). Erickson family panel: The child-rearing techniques of Milton Erickson. In J. K. Zeig (Ed.), *Ericksonian psychotherapy: Volume 1: structures* (pp. 619-637). New York: Brunner/Mazel.

Gordon, D. & Meyers-Anderson, M. (1981). *Phoenix: Therapeutic patterns of Milton H. Erickson.* Cupertino, CA: Meta.

Haley, J. (1973). *Uncommon therapy.* New York: Norton.

Haley, J. (1993). *Jay Haley on Milton H. Erickson.* New York: Brunner/Mazel.

Howell, K.W. & Nolet, V. (2000). *Curriculum-based evaluation, teaching and decision making* (3rd ed, p. 390). Pacific Grove, CA: Wadsworth.

Lankton, C.H. (1985). Generative change: Beyond symptomatic relief. In J.K. Zeig (Ed.), *Ericksonian psychotherapy: Volume 1: structures* (pp. 137-170). New York: Brunner/Mazel.

Maag, J.W. (1997). Managing resistance: Remembering how to fly a kite. *Reclaiming Children and Youth: Journal of Emotional and Behavioral Problems, 6*(2), 114-119.

Mastropieri, M.A. & Scruggs, T.E. (1994). *Effective instruction for special education* (2nd ed.). Austin, TX: Pro-Ed.

Premack, D. (1959). Toward empirical behavioral laws: I Positive reinforcement, *Psychological Review, 66*, 219-233.

Rhode, G., Jenson, W.R. & Reavis, H.K. (1995). *The tough kid book: Practical classroom management strategies* (5th ed.). Longmont, CO: Sopris West.

Rosen, S. (1982). *My voice will go with you: The teaching tales of Milton H. Erickson.* New York: Norton.

Zeig, J.K. (Ed.). (1985). *Ericksonian psychotherapy: Volume 1: structures.* New York: Brunnere/Mazel.

Part III: Function Over Form

Ayllon, T. (1963). Intensive treatment of psychotic behavior by stimulus satiation and food reinforcement. *Behavior Research and Therapy, 1*, 53-61.

Dunlap, G. & Kern, L. (1993). Assessment and intervention for children within the instructional curriculum. In J. Reichle & D. Wacker (Eds.), *Communication alternatives to challenging behavior: Integrating functional assessment and intervention strategies*, (pp. 177-203). Baltimore: Brookes.

Foster-Johnson, L. & Dunlap, G. (1993). Using functional assessment to develop effective, individualized interventions for challenging behaviors. *Teaching Exceptional Children, 25* (3), 44-50.

Foster-Johnson, L. & Dunlap, G. (1993). Using functional assessment to develop effective, individualized interventions for challenging behaviors. *Teaching Exceptional Children, 25* (3), p.48.

Hallahan, D.P., Lloyd, J.W. & Stoller, L. (1982). *Improving attention with self-monitoring.* Charlottesville, VA: University of Virginia Learning Disabilities Research Institute.

Jenson, W.R., Andrews, D. & Reavis, K. (1992). *Good behavior pool. Best times.* Salt Lake City, UT: Utah State Office of Education.

Kaplan, J.S. (1995). *Beyond behavior modification: A cognitive-behavioral approach to behavior management in the school* (3rd ed.). Austin, TX: Pro-Ed.

Larson, P.J. & Maag, J.W. (1998). Applying functional assessment in general education classrooms: Issues and recommendations. *Remedial and Special Education*, 19, 338-349.

Levitt, L.K. & Rutherford, R.B. (1978) *Strategies for handling the disruptive student.* Tempe, AZ: College of Education, Arizona State University.

Maag, J.W. (1996). *Parenting without punishment: Making problem behavior work for you.* Philadelphia, PA: The Charles Press.

Morris, W. (Ed.) (1976). *The American Heritage Dictionary of the English Language.* Boston: Houghton Mifflin Company.

Neel, R.S. & Cessna, K.K. (1993). Behavioral intent: Instructional content for students with behavior disorders. In K.K. Cessna (Ed.), *Instructionally differentiated programming: A needs-based approach for students with behavior disorders* (pp. 31-39). Denver, CO: Colorado Department of Education.

Premack, D. (1959). Toward empirical behavioral laws: I Positive reinforcement, *Psychological Review, 66,* 219-233.

Rhode, G., Jenson, W.R. & Reavis, H.K. (1992). *The tough kid book: Practical classroom management strategies* (5th ed.). Longmont, CO: Sopris West.

Rosen, S. (1982). *My voice will go with you: The teaching tales of Milton H. Erickson.* New York: Norton.

Part IV: Changing Our Behavior

Anderson, C.M. & Stewart, S. (1983). *Mastering resistance: A practical guide to family therapy.* New York: Guilford.

Bandler, R. & Grinder, J. (1975). *Patterns of the hypnotic techniques of Milton H. Erickson, M.D* (Vol. 1) Capitola, CA: Meta.

Bandler, R. & Grinder, J. (1982). *Reframing: Neuro-linguistic programming and the transformation of meaning.* Moab, UT: Real People Press.

Barker, J.A. (1992). *Paradigms: The business of discovering the future.* New York: Harper Collins.

Cormier, W.H. & Cormier, L.S. (1985). *Interviewing strategies for helpers: Fundamental skills and cognitive behavioral interventions* (2nd ed.). Monterey, CA: Brooks/Cole.

Dryden, W. & DiGiuseppe, R. (1990). *A primer on rational-emotive therapy.* Champaign, IL: Research Press.

Ellis, A. (1962). *Reason and emotion in psychotherapy.* New York: Stuart.

Erickson, M.H. (1962). The identification of a secure family. *Family Process, 1,* 294-303.

Fisch, R., Weakland, J. & Segal, L. (1982). *The tactics of change: Doing therapy briefly*. San Francisco: Jossey-Bass.

Gordon, D. & Meyers-Anderson, M. (1981). *Phoenix: Therapeutic patterns of Milton H. Erickson*. Cupertino, CA: Meta.

Gordon, D. (1978). *Therapeutic metaphors*. Cupertino, CA: META Publications.

Haley, J. (1973). *Uncommon therapy*. New York: Norton.

Haley, J. (1984). *Ordeal therapy*. San Francisco, CA: Jossey-Bass.

Hassenpflug, A. (1983). Insanity in the classroom. *English Journal, 72*(8), 33-34.

Maag, J.W. (1996). *Parenting without punishment: Making problem behavior work for you*. Philadelphia, PA: The Charles Press.

Maag, J.W. (1997). Managing resistance: Remembering how to fly a kite. *Journal of Emotional and Behavioral Problems*, 6, 114-119.

Maag, J.W. (1999). *Behavior management: From theoretical implications to practical applications*. San Diego: Singular Press.

Miller, T. (1986). *The unfair advantage*. Skaneateles, NY: Lakeside.

Rosen, S. (1982). *My voice will go with you: The teaching tales of Milton H. Erickson*. New York: Norton.

Rossi, E.L., Ryan, M.O. & Sharp, F.A. (Eds.). (1983). *Healing in hypnosis: The seminars, workshops, and lectures of Milton H. Erickson* (Vol. 1). New York: Irvington.

Watzlawick, P., Weakland, J. & Fisch, R. (1974). *Change: Principles of problem formation and problem resolution*. New York: Norton.

Reproducibles

Larson, P.J. & Maag, J.W. (1998). Applying functional assessment in general education classrooms: Issues and recommendations. *Remedial and Special Education, 19*, 338-346. Austin, TX: Pro-Ed.

REPRODUCIBLES

Functional Assessment Hypotheses Formulation Protocol

Student: _____

Dates: _____

Behavior: _____

Observer(s): _____

I. BEHAVIOR DEFINITION

Definition Components

Operationally defining the problem behavior is the first step in conducting an effective functional assessment. In order to arrive at a reliable definition that can observed and measured, answer the following questions:

1. What does the problem behavior look like? Check the behavior that is of greatest concern.

___ Aggression   ___ Out of seat/place

___ Destruction of property   ___ Tardy/late to class

___ Excessive movement/fidgeting   ___ Talks out/disrupts class

___ Inappropriate language   ___ Theft

___ Insubordination   ___ Threatening
___ Not completing work   ___ Other (specify) _____

2. How is the behavior performed (topography)? Consider the type of physical movement and the use of objects:

_____

_____

3. How long does behavior last when it occurs (duration)? Check box that corresponds to the approximate length of time and circle the appropriate time measurement.

___ 1 - 2 seconds/minutes   ___ 15 - 20 seconds/minutes

___ 3 - 5 seconds/minutes   ___ 20 - 25 seconds/minutes

___ 5 -10 seconds/minutes   ___ 25 - 30 seconds/minutes
___ 10 - 15 seconds/minutes   ___ Other _____

4. How often does the behavior occur (frequency)? *Indicate the rate of occurrence using the following formula. (For example, 3 or 4 times per hour.)* _____ times per _____.

5. How damaging or destructive is the behavior (intensity)? *For example, no physical injury.*

_____

_____

6. Where does the behavior occur and who is typically involved (setting)?

_____

_____

Definition Summary

Using the answers to the preceding questions, write an operational definition of the target behavior. For example: During transition periods when new students are present, Jane uses aggression by striking peers with an open hand on the back for one to two seconds, three or four times a period, with no physical injury.

_____

_____

_____

II. FACTOR IDENTIFICATION

Setting Events

Using the following checklists, identify the factors that usually occur prior to or as a result of the target behavior.

1. Factors that appear to set off and/or precede the target behavior:

Teacher Behaviors

_____Encouragement/praise

_____Independent work/lack of attention

_____Individual attention to student

_____Lesson presentation/lecture

_____Performance feedback/evaluation

_____Reprimand

_____Task explanation/demand

Environmental Factors

_____Access/availability of food

_____Access/availability of preferred task/activity

_____Elevated/excessive noise levels

_____Presence of unusual/extra adult(s)

_____Presence of unusual/extra peer(s)

_____Termination of preferred task/activity

_____Transition task/activity (expected/routine)

_____Transition task/activity (unexpected/irregular)

Student Behaviors

_____Disturbed affect (sad, angry appearance)

_____Drowsy/sleepy appearance

_____Excessive motor activity (fidgety, restless)

_____Peer attention (negative)

_____Peer attention (positive)

_____Physical complaints (hunger, pain, etc.)

2. Factors that appear to maintain/follow the occurrence of problem behavior:

Teacher Behaviors

_____Encouragement/praise

_____Reprimand

_____Task removal

_____Withdrawal of attention/ignoring

Student Behaviors

_____Peer attention (negative)

_____Withdrawal of peer attention/isolation

Environmental Factors

_____Access/availability of preferred activity/task

_____Removal of student to alternative setting

Behavioral Intent Identification

Using the following checklist, identify the possible functions or outcomes that the target behavior may serve for the student. If more than one function appears to be a reasonable explanation, rank order your responses from 1 to 3, with 1 being the most likely function of the behavior.

___ Acceptance/affiliation/approval   ___Gratification ___

___ Attention   ___ Justice/revenge

___ Escape/avoid task/event   ___ Power/control

___ Escape/avoid attention   ___ Sensory stimulation

___ Expression of self   ___ Tangible reward

___ Gain access to objects/activities   ___ Other _____

III. OBSERVATION

Student: _____ Dates: _____

Target Behavior: _____

Observer _____

X = 3 or more occurrences   **O** = 1 or 2 occurrences

Activity	Time	Days									
		M	T	W	Th	F	M	T	W	Th	F

IV. FUNCTIONAL HYPOTHESIS

Hypothesis Statement

Using the information from Sections I, II, and III, construct a hypothesis statement by filling in the blanks.

When _____

(identify setting events)

_____ will _____

(student)   (behavior)

in order to _____

(intended outcome/function)

Functional Analysis Plan

In order to test the hypothesis, the following functional analysis will be implemented.

1. Contextual Modification: What changes in environment/and or teacher behaviors will be attempted?

_____

_____

_____

2. Curricular Accommodation: What changes in instructional materials/techniques will be attempted?

_____

_____

_____

3. Replacement Strategy: What new behaviors/strategies will be taught?

_____

_____

_____

Frequency Recording Sheet

Student: _____

Date: _____

Observer _____ Time Began: _____

Time Ended: _____

Target Behavior: _____

_____

Date	Time Start/Stop	Notations of Occurrences	Total Occurrences

Duration Recording Sheet

Student: _____

Date: _____

Observer _____   Time Began: _____

                                        Time Ended: _____

Target Behavior: _____

_____

Date	Time		Duration
	Behavior Begins	**Behavior Ends**	

5-Minute Interval Recording Sheet

Student: _____

Date:_____

Observer:_____   Time Began: _____

Time Ended: _____

Target Behavior: _____

_____

Directions: Place an "X" in the interval boxes in which the target behavior occurred and a "O" in the interval boxes in which the target behavior did not occur.

Total Observation Time Equals 5 Minutes

	Seconds	Seconds	Seconds	Seconds	Seconds
___Minute					
___Minutes					
___Minutes					
___Minutes					
___Minutes					
___Minutes					
___Minute					
___Minutes					
___Minutes					
___Minutes					

Percentage of intervals student engaged in the target behavior_____%

Self-Monitoring Card

Name _____ Date _____

When you hear the beep, ask yourself if you are:

If the answer is yes to any of these, place a check in the **"Yes"** column.
If the answer is no, place a check in the **"No"** column.

	YES	NO		YES	NO
1.			13.		
2.			14.		
3.			15.		
4.			16.		
5.			17.		
6.			18.		
7.			19.		
8.			20.		
9.			21.		
10.			22.		
11.			23.		
12.			24.		
			TOTALS		

Self-Monitoring Card

Name _____ Date _____

When you hear the beep, ask yourself if you are:

If the answer is yes to any of these, place a check in the **"Yes"** column.
If the answer is no, place a check in the **"No"** column.

	YES	NO		YES	NO
1.			13.		
2.			14.		
3.			15.		
4.			16.		
5.			17.		
6.			18.		
7.			19.		
8.			20.		
9.			21.		
10.			22.		
11.			23.		
12.			24.		
			TOTALS		

Self-Monitoring Card

Name _____ **Date** _____

When you hear the beep, ask yourself if you are:

If the answer is yes to any of these, place a check in the ☺ column.
If the answer is no, place a check in the ☹ column.

	☺	☹
1.		
2.		
3.		
4.		
5.		
6.		
7.		
8.		
9.		
10.		
11.		
12.		

	☺	☹
13.		
14.		
15.		
16.		
17.		
18.		
19.		
20.		
21.		
22.		
23.		
24.		
TOTALS		

Self-Monitoring Card

Name _____ **Date** _____

When you hear the beep, ask yourself if you are:

If the answer is yes to any of these, place a check in the ☺ column.
If the answer is no, place a check in the ☹ column.

	☺	☹
1.		
2.		
3.		
4.		
5.		
6.		
7.		
8.		
9.		
10.		
11.		
12.		

	☺	☹
13.		
14.		
15.		
16.		
17.		
18.		
19.		
20.		
21.		
22.		
23.		
24.		
TOTALS		

Self-Monitoring Card

Make a mark beside the day of the week every time you follow a direction without being told twice.

		Total
Monday		
Tuesday		
Wednesday		
Thursday		
Friday		
Grand Total		

Name _____ Date _____

Self-Monitoring Card

Make a mark beside the day of the week every time you follow a direction without being told twice.

		Total
Monday		
Tuesday		
Wednesday		
Thursday		
Friday		
Grand Total		

Name _____ Date _____

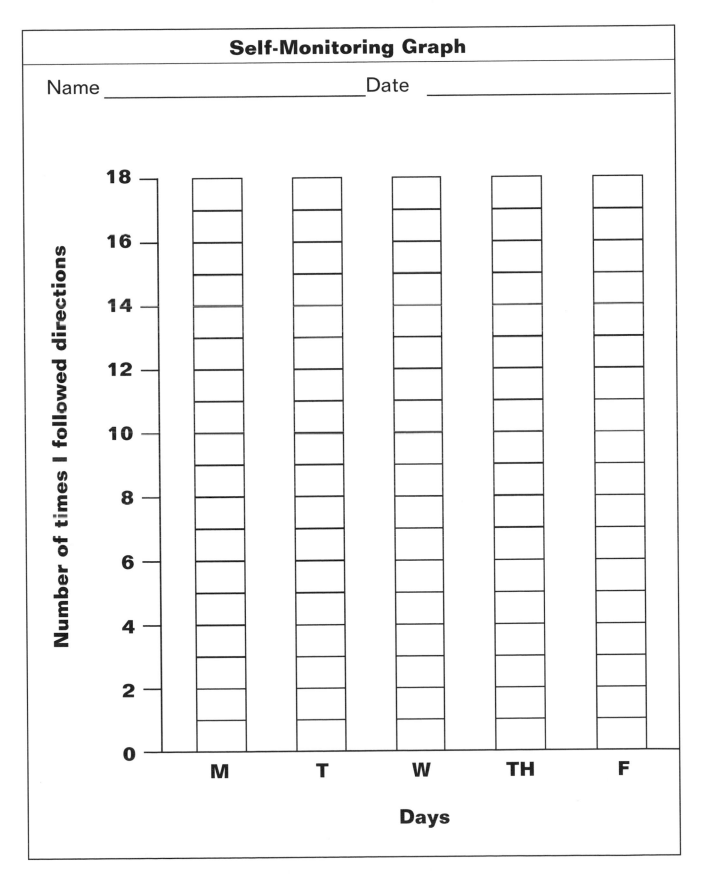

Self-Monitoring Graph

Name _____ Date _____

Number of times I followed directions

18
16
14
12
10
8
6
4
2
0

M   T   W   TH   F

Days

Matrix X

1	2	3
4	5	6
7	8	9

Matrix Y

1	2	3	4
5	6	7	8
9	10	11	12
13	14	15	16

Winning Compliance Matrices

Matrix Z

1	2	3	4	5
6	7	8	9	10
11	12	13	14	15
16	17	18	19	20
21	22	23	24	25

Chart Moves Reinforcement Program

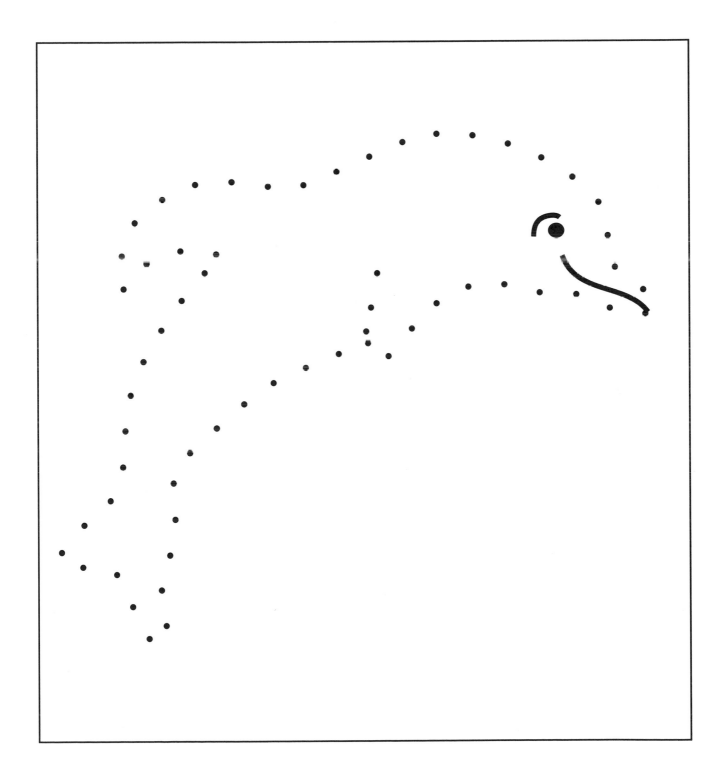

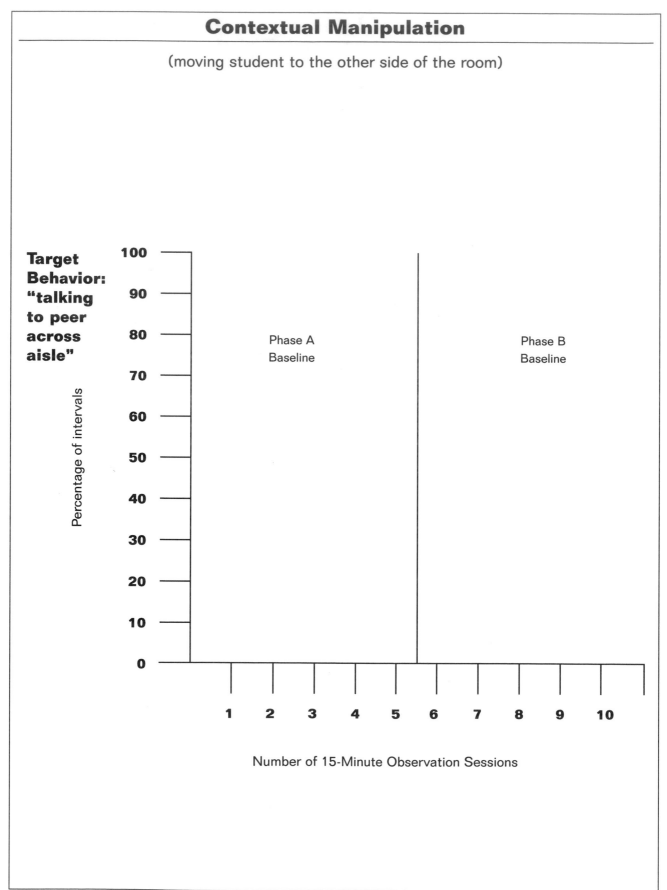

Contextual Manipulation

(moving student to the other side of the room)

Target Behavior: "talking to peer across aisle"

Percentage of intervals

100
90
80
70
60
50
40
30
20
10
0

Phase A Baseline

Phase B Baseline

1   2   3   4   5   6   7   8   9   10

Number of 15-Minute Observation Sessions

Recording a Self-Monitoring Tape

Materials Needed: Slips of paper, a separate sheet of paper, a pen, a tape recorder and tape, instrument or object for making the tone, and a clock with a second hand.

A variety of objects can be used to produce the auditory tone: tapping a glass with a spoon, striking a piano key, or pushing a button on a phone. There are also many electronic devices that emit tones, such as touchtone phones.

Students must not be able to determine the amount of time that passes between tones. Random tones ensure that students continue to perform the compliant behaviors at a high frequency or for a long duration. For a lesson of 15 to 20 minutes, tone intervals should average 45 seconds and range from 10 seconds (the shortest interval) to 90 seconds (the longest interval). These figures may be doubled for work periods lasting 30 to 40 minutes (inter-tone average of 90 seconds with a range of 20 to 180 seconds). When the average inter-tone interval and range have been decided, a list of random intervals can be produced as follows:

1. Write the numbers of each possible interval length on slips of paper and place them in a container. For a tape averaging tones every 45 seconds, you would write: 10 seconds, 11 seconds, 12 seconds, etc. For a tape averaging tones every 90 seconds, you would write numbers from 20 seconds to 180 seconds.

2. Draw a slip of paper from the container and write down the number.

3. Place the slip of paper back in the container so that each number has an equal chance of being drawn every time.

4. For a 20-minute tape, repeat this process until 20 numbers have been picked. For a 40-minute tape, repeat this process until 40 numbers have been picked.

5. Now you are ready to record the self-monitoring tape. Find a quiet room and let the tape play for the number of seconds indicated by the first number on your list. At this time, record the signal tone. Then let the tape recorder play for the amount of time indicated by the second number on your interval list. Then record the signal tone. Check off each interval on your list as you record it. Repeat the process until the end of the tape.

Related Sources from Sopris West

Get 'Em on Task

A Computer Signaling Program to Teach Attending and Self-Management Skills

R. Brad Althouse; William Jenson, Ph.D.; Marilyn Likins, Ph.D.; and Daniel Morgan, Ph.D.

Grades K–12

You can use this auditory signaling system with any self-management program. Step-by-step instructions make it easy to set program length, number of signals, random or regular/specific intervals, and even "bonus" signals. 3.5 PC disk. Minimum requirements: Windows® 3.1 or later, 386 PC, 8 MB RAM, 4 MG hard drive, sound card.

The Tough Kid Book

Practical Classroom Management Strategies

Ginger Rhode, Ph.D.; William R. Jenson, Ph.D.; and H. Kenton Reavis, Ed.D.

These ready-to-use, research-validated solutions will help you reduce disruptive behavior and make your classroom pleasant and productive. Includes step-by-step strategies to deal with aggression, arguing, tantrums, poor academic progress, and more.

The Tough Kid Tool Box

William R. Jenson, Ph.D.; Ginger Rhode, Ph.D.; and H. Kenton Reavis, Ed.D.

These timesaving, engaging student reproducibles will enable you to implement the positive behavior management strategies of *The Tough Kid Book*—without the extra effort. Includes Behavior Observation Forms, Mystery Motivator Charts, Reward Spinners, Contracts, and more. Step-by-step instructions make each reproducible immediately useful.

The Acting-Out Child

Coping With Classroom Disruption

Hill M. Walker, Ph.D.

Grades K–6

Gain a thorough understanding of acting-out behavior—its origins and development, why common attempts to cope with inappropriate behavior fail, which strategies really do work, how to assess behavior, how best to combine interventions, how to defuse oppositional and aggressive behavior, and more. This comprehensive second edition of the Walker classic provides case studies, model interventions, and suggestions for how to reintegrate acting-out students into general education classrooms.

Workshop Available

For more information, please call us at (800) 547-6747, or visit our website www.sopriswest.com.

Index

Note: Page numbers followed by the letter "f" indicate figures; those followed by the letter "t" indicate tables; those that are italicized indicate reproducibles.

A

A-B-C model of behavior, 54ft-55, 86

acceptance vs. approval, 110-111

accuracy, and skill proficiency, 27

acne, 119-120

alcoholism, 131

alpha commands, ix

always-and-never thinking, 108

analogical behavior, 18

Anderson, C.M., 123

Andrews, D., 71

Andy Griffith Show, The, 21-22

anecdotes, as metaphor strategy, 133

antecedent manipulations, 55, 57-66.
See also manipulation

antecedents, 39, 53. See also consequences

approach-approach conflict, 48

approach-avoidance conflict, 48

Attention Deficit Hyperactivity Disorder (ADHD), 22

automaticity, and skill proficiency, 27

avoidance-avoidance conflict, 48

awfulizing, 108, 111-113

Ayllon, T., 14, 61, 85

Azrin, N.H., 30-31

B

Bandler, R.
on elegance, 142
on embedding, 33
on frame of reference, 134
on meaning reframing, 135-136
on pacing, 16, 17

Barker, J.A., 99

bed-wetting, 116, 126-127

beeper tape, 59, 80, 81. *See also* Recording a
Self-Monitoring Tape

behavior
A-B-C model, 54-55, 86
analogical, 18
cant or wont model of resistance, 23-25
changing patterns of, 61-66
cognitive model, 39-41
defining target, 87-88
determining function of, 85-96, 149-150
direct observation of, 88-89
effect of context on, 12-14
effect of sense stimuli on, 39-40
high/low probability, 35-36, 74-75
impact of environment on, 53-55, 88
matching students, 16-18
not taking personally, 102
passive, 64-66
physical aspects of, 119-120
problem, used as reinforcer, 75-78
small changes in, 44-47
social norms and standards for, 21-22
strategies for controlling ones own, 105-114
topography, 119-120
use of humor to change, 144-145

behavior reduction techniques, 29

behavioral intent, 14, 86t

behavioral momentum, 35-36

behavioral view of resistance, 12

beliefs

  effect on perception, 3

  irrational, 39-41, 107-113

  pessimistic, 41-47

  rational, 39

  as Type 2 Prerequisites, 23-24, 25

beta commands, ix

Beyer, J.K., 48

Boring, E.G., 4, 5f

C

Cameron-Bandler, Leslie, 135-136

cant or wont model of resistance, 23-24f

Cessna, K.K., 14, 86

change, striving for small, 44-47

Chart Moves reinforcement program, 71f-72, 83, *171*

cognitive dissonance, 48

cognitive model of behavior, 39f-41

Colvin, G., ix

compliance, 9

Compliance Matrix, 70-71. *See also* Winning
  Compliance Matrices

compliance-based paradoxes, 117-122.
  See also defiance-based paradoxes;
  paradoxical directives

    ordeal therapy, 120-122

    scheduling, 117-119

    topography, 119-120

conflict, 48

consequences, 39, 53-54, 67, 68.
  See also antecedents

consequent manipulations, 55, 67-83.
  See also manipulation

consistency, 40, 101

contagion concern, 34

context

  effect on behavior, 61, 63-64

  role in managing resistance, 12-14, 28

context reframing, 136-138

contextual hypotheses, 86-87. *See also* hypotheses

contextual manipulation, 12-14, 93f, 149, *172*.
  See also manipulation

contingencies, 53

control. *See* power and control

Coren, S., 4f

Cormier, L.S., ix, 124

Cormier, W.H., ix, 124

covert metaphors, 131-132. *See also* therapeutic
  metaphors

cross-over mirroring, 18

curricular hypotheses, 87

curricular manipulation, 93f

D

damnation, 108

defiance-based paradoxes, 122-124

  giving in directive, 123-124

  hard restraining, 124

  relapse prediction, 124

  slow down directive, 122-123

demandingness, 108-111

dependent group-oriented contingency, 81-82.
  See also interdependent group-oriented
  contingency

destructive behavior, 140-141

DiGiuseppe, R., 108

direct skill training, 28

discipline vs. punishment, 68

domino effect, 12f-13

do-nothing chair strategy, 64-66, 95, 119

double bind, Ericksons childhood use of, 7-8

Dryden, W., 108

Dunlap, G., 88, 89

duration recording, 91

Duration Recording Sheet, 91, *162*

E

elegance, 142

Ellis, A., 39, 105, 107-108

embedding instructions, 33-35

emotional overpayment, 112-113

emotions, strategies for controlling ones own,
    105-114

environment, impact on behavior, 23, 53-55, 88

Erickson, A., 43

Erickson, K.K., 43

Erickson, L., 43

Erickson, Milton H.

    acknowledging pessimism, 42-43

    biographical sketch, 7-8

    on death, 113

    development of strategic therapy, x

    establishing rapport, 16-17

    and I really dont care attitude, 30

    river analogy, 115-116

    seeding ideas, 44

    and small change, 46

    techniques used by

        embedding, 33

        frame of reference, 116

        humor, 144-145

        inconvenience approach, 32-33

        meaning reframing, 135, 139-140

        negative practice, 31-32

        ordeal therapy, 120-121

        pacing, 17-18

        paradoxical intervention, 7-8

        pattern reversal, 62-64

        scheduling, 118-119

        surprise and shock technique, 140-141, 142

        therapeutic metaphor, 126-127, 131

        topography, 119-120

        unconventional interventions, 101

Erickson, R., 43

Erickson-Klein, R., 43

experience, and rational-emotive therapy, 105-107

F

fairytale metaphors, 132-133

family systems view of resistance, 11-12, 102

field theory, 47-48

figure-ground perception, 4

Fisch, R., 101, 122, 123

5-Minute Interval Recording Sheet, *163*

fluency, and skill proficiency, 27

force-field analysis, 47f-50

form, and use of punishment, 68

49 Square Chart reinforcement program, 73f-74,
    81, 83

Foster-Johnson, L., 89

frame of reference, 16, 117, 134

Frantz, S.E., 30-31

frequency recording, 90-91

Frequency Recording Sheet, 91, *161*

Freud, Sigmund, 10-11, 102

function, and use of punishment, 68

functional analysis, 90

Functional Assessment Hypotheses Formulation
    Protocol, 89, 90, *157-160*

functional assessments, 85-96

    hypothesis development, 87-90

hypothesis testing, 90-96

recording methods, 90-93

functional hypotheses, 86. *See also* hypotheses

functional manipulation, 94f. *See also* manipulation

G

Gestalt psychologists, on effect of paradigms, 4

giving in directive, 123-124

goals, well-formed, 129

Good Behavior Game, 80, 81f, 82-83

Gordon, D.

on guiding fantasies, 133-134

on humor, 144

on making small changes, 46

on matching predicates, 18

on metaphors, 127-128, 130, 132

on personal worldviews, 15

on reframing, 135, 138, 140

on stories, 126

Grab-Bag, 36

Grinder, J.

on elegance, 142

on embedding, 33

on frame of reference, 134

on meaning reframing, 135-136

on pacing, 16, 17

group-oriented contingencies, 81-83

guided fantasies, as metaphor strategy, 133-134

guided practice, and skill proficiency, 27

H

Haley, J.

on difficulty of describing Ericksons work, x

on Ericksons ability to seed ideas, 44

on Ericksons afflictions, 7

on Ericksons river analogy, 115

on Ericksons use of different techniques

acknowledging pessimism, 42-43

frames of reference, 116

therapeutic metaphors, 126

on ordeal therapy, 120, 121

Hallahan, D.P., 58

hard restraining, 124

Hassenpflug, A., 142-143

Hero Procedure, 81-82

high probability behavior, 35-36, 74-75

hoarding behavior, 14

homeostasis, 12

Homme, Lloyd, 75

Howell, K.W., 23, 24f

humor, 144-145

hyperactivity, 22-23

hypnosis, 8

hypotheses

contextual, 86-87

curricular, 87

development of, 87-90

functional, 86

testing of, 90-96, 95

I

I can't stand it! Its awful! (low frustration tolerance), 108, 113

ideomotor principle of hypnosis, 8

inconvenience approach, 32-33

independent practice, and skill proficiency, 27

input channels, 16

insanity, as classroom management strategy, 142-143

insomnia, 135

instructions, embedding, 33-35

interdependent group-oriented contingency, 82-83.
See also dependent group-oriented contingency
interval recording, 91, 92-93
Interval Recording Sheet, 92, 93, *163*
irrational beliefs, 39-41, 107-113

J

Jenson, W.R., 35, 36, 37, 70, 71, 72
judgment, biased, 103

K

Kaplan, J.S., 87
Kern, L., 88
Kuhn, T.S., 4

L

Larson, P.J., 90, 157-160, 161, 162, 163
Levitt, L.K., 75
Lewin, Kurt, 47-48
limitations, overcoming, 99-103
linear interventions, 101, 102
Lloyd, J.W., 58
low probability behavior, 35-36, 75

M

Maag, J.W.
    5-Minute Interval Recording Sheet, 163
    on acknowledging pessimism, 41, 42
    on consistency, 101
    Duration Recording Sheet, 162
    Frequency Recording Sheet, 161
    on functional assessment, 90
    Functional Assessment Hypotheses
        Formulation Protocol, 157-160
    on Good Behavior Game, 82
    on group-oriented contingencies, 81
    on negative practice, 31
    on paradigm paralysis, 5-6
    on problem behaviors as reinforcers, 75-76
    on punishment, 101
    on trying to force compliance, 116
manipulation
    antecedent, 57-66
    consequent, 67-83
    contextual, 12-14, 93, 149, 172
    curricular, 93
    functional, 94
    role in managing resistance, 13-14
Mastropieri, M.A., 27
meaning reframing, 135-136
medical-disease model of resistance, 21-23
metaphors. See therapeutic metaphors
Meyers-Anderson, M.
    on humor, 144
    on making small changes, 46
    on matching predicates, 18
    on personal worldviews, 15
    on reframing, 135, 138, 140
Miller, T., 108, 112, 113
mirroring, 18
modalities, sensory, 18
momentum, building, 33-37
Mom's Rule, 75. See also Premack principle
My friend John metaphors, 132
Mystery Motivators, 36, 83
    reinforcement program, 72

N

Neel, R.S., 14, 86
negative practice, 30-32. See also ordeal therapy
Nolet, V., 23, 24f
noncompliance, 9

noncompliant behaviors, viewed as disorders, 21-23

Nunn, R.G., 30-31

O

observation, 18, 88-89, 93-96

Obsessive-Compulsive Disorder (OCD), 119, 135-136

Oppositional Defiant Disorder, 21, 22t

ordeal therapy, 120-122t. *See also* negative practice

output channels, 16

overcorrection, 28-29

overt metaphors, 132-134. *See also* therapeutic
    metaphors

P

pacing, 16f-18

pantomime technique, 18

Paracelsus, 120

paradigm paralysis, 4-5, 99, 147

paradigms, 3-8, 99-100

paradoxical directives, 115-126

    cautions when using, 124-126

    compliance-based paradoxes, 117-122

    defiance-based paradoxes, 122-124

paradoxical injunction, 46

paradoxical intervention, Ericksons childhood use
    of, 7-8

passivity, 64-66, 95-96

pattern reversal, 62-64

patterns of behavior, changing, 61-66

patterns of responding, 103

peer pressure, and group-oriented contingencies, 83

peers, reinforcing, 79-81

perception psychologists, on effect of paradigms, 4

person-centered counseling approach, and rapport, 15

pessimism, acknowledging, 41-47

physical injury scale, 111f, 112-114

Porac, C., 4f

positive practice overcorrection, 29-30

positive reinforcement, 67-70

postural congruence, 18

power and control

    and passivity, 95

    reinforcing value of, 29-30

    and sabotage, 83

    students' attempts to gain, 6-7, 13, 16, 64-66,
        76-77, 116

power struggle, avoiding, 29, 30

practice techniques for managing resistance, 28-33

predicates, matching, 18

Premack, D., 49, 75

Premack principle, 49, 75

prerequisites, for selecting behavior, 23-25

problem behaviors, used as reinforcers, 75-78

punishment

    definition, 68-69

    overcorrection as form of, 28-29

    and reinforcement, 69-70

    rewards functioning as, 69

    vs. discipline, 68

Q

quotes, as metaphor strategy, 133

R

Ramsey, E., ix

rapport, 15-18, 41, 42, 117, 148

rational beliefs, 39

Rational-Emotive Therapy (RET), 39, 105-114

reactivity, and self-monitoring, 58

Reavis, H.K., 35, 36, 37, 70, 71, 72

Recording a Self-Monitoring Tape, 59, 80, 81-82, *173*

recording methods for functional assessment, 90-93

reframing, 115, 134-140
    of context, 136-138
    five steps of, 138-140
    of meaning, 135-136
reinforcement
    avoiding burnout, 78
    individual nature of, 74-78
    of peers, 79f-81
    positive, 67-70
    reducing competing sources of, 78-83
reinforcement programs, 71-74
reinforcers
    choosing effective, 70-71
    problem behaviors used as, 75-78
relapse prediction, 124
replacement behavior, 14, 85, 86
reproducibles
    Chart Moves Reinforcement Program, *171*
    Contextual Manipulation, *172*
    Duration Recording Sheet, *162*
    Frequency Recording Sheet, *161*
    Functional Assessment Hypotheses
        Formulation Protocol, *157-160*
    Interval Recording Sheet, *163*
    "Recording a Self-Monitoring Tape," *173*
    Self-Monitoring Cards, *164, 165, 166*
    Self-Monitoring Graph, *167*
    Winning Compliance Matrices, *168, 169, 170*
resistance
    advanced approaches for managing, 115-145
        paradoxical directives, 115-126
        reframing, 134-140
        surprise and shock technique, 140-145
        therapeutic metaphors, 126-134
    becoming cooperation, 116-117

behavioral view, 12
cant or wont model, 23-24
definition, 9
family systems view, 11-12, 102
Freudian view, 10-11, 102
medical-disease model, 21-23
and paradigms, 4-7
practice techniques for managing, 28-33
rationale for using term, ix
using to obtain compliance, 148-149
response cost, and Sure I Will program, 36
response, unconventional, 102-103
restitutional overcorrection, 28-29
rewards, functioning as punishments, 69
Rhode, G., 35, 36, 37, 70, 71, 72
risk, fear of, as factor in resistance, 11-12
Rogers, Carl, 15
Roseanne, 21-22
Rosen, S.
    on Ericksons use of different techniques
        meaning reframing, 139
        negative practice, 31
        pattern reversal, 62
        rapport, 16-17
        scheduling, 118
        surprise and shock technique, 140
        therapeutic metaphor, 131
        topography, 119
Rossi, E.L., 7, 101
routines, changing, 61-66
Rubin, Edgar, 4
Rubin vase, as example of figure-ground
    perception, 4f
Rutherford, R.B., 75
Ryan, M.O., 7, 101

S

sabotage, and group-oriented contingencies, 83

satiation, and reinforcement, 78

Satir, Virginia, 136-137

scapegoating, and group-oriented contingencies, 82t, 83

scatter plot, 89f

scheduling, 117-119

schemas, 39-41, 108-109, 142

Scruggs, T.E., 27

seeding ideas, 42

Segal, L., 122

self-monitoring

    cards for, 59f-60, *164, 165, 166*

    cues for, 59-61

    graph for, 60f-61, *167*

    procedures for, 62

    teaching, 57-60

self-monitoring attention (SMA), 58-59

sense stimuli, effect on behavior, 39-40

sensory modalities, 18

sequence confusion, 45f, 46

Sharp, F.A., 7, 101

skills

    direct training of, 28

    helping students who lack, 27-37

    as Type 1 Prerequisites, 23

slow down directive, 122-123

Spinners reinforcement program, 72f-73, 81, 83

Stewart, S., 123

stimuli, sense, effect on behavior, 39-40

stimulus saturation, 61-62

stimulus-response chain, 46, 61

Stoller, L., 58

stories, metaphorical, strategies for telling, 130-131

Stranger Test, for defining target behavior, 87-88

strategic therapy, x

strategies, for selecting behavior, 24

structural equivalence, 128

Structure of Scientific Revolutions, The (Kuhn), 4

Sure I Will program, 36f-37

surprise and shock technique, 115, 140-145

swearing, 12-13, 77

T

target behavior, 87-88

teachers, tolerance levels of, 22-23

therapeutic metaphors, 115, 126-134

    constructing, 127-130

    covert, 131-132

    fairytales, 132-133

    overt, 132-134

    strategies for telling stories, 130-131

thumbsucking, 120-121

time sampling, 91, 92-93

tolerance levels, of teachers, 22-23

topography, 119-120

towers, in Chart Moves reinforcement program, 72

Type 1 Prerequisites, 23-24, 27-37

Type 2 Prerequisites, 23-24, 25, 39-50

W

Walker, H.M., ix

Ward, L.M., 4f

Watzlawick, P., 101, 123

Weakland, J., 101, 122, 123

Winning Compliance Matrices, 70f, *168, 169, 170*

Z

Zeig, J.K., 8, 30, 32